DO
NOTHING
TO CHANGE
YOUR LIFE

DISCOVERING
WHAT HAPPENS
WHEN YOU STOP

STEPHEN COTTRELL

CHURCH HOUSE
PUBLISHING

Church House Publishing
Church House
Great Smith Street
London SW1P 3NZ

Tel: 020 7898 1451
Fax: 020 7898 1449

ISBN 978-0-7151-4118-2

Published 2007 by Church House Publishing
Copyright © Stephen Cottrell 2007

The opinions expressed in this book are those of the author
and do not necessarily reflect the official policy of the General
Synod or The Archbishops' Council of the Church of England.

Printed in England by Cromwell Press Ltd, Trowbridge, Wiltshire

Life is not hurrying
on to a receding future, nor hankering after
an imagined past. It is the turning
aside like Moses to the miracle
of the lit bush, to a brightness
that seemed as transitory as your youth
once, but is the eternity that awaits you.

R. S. Thomas, *The Bright Field*

Why is it so hard to quickly sum up all of those things that we have learned while being alive here on Earth? Why can't I just tell you, 'In ten minutes you are going to be hit by a bus, and so in those ten minutes you must quickly itemise what you have learned from being alive.' Chances are that you would have a blank list. And even if you gave the matter the greatest concentration, you would still have a blank list. And yet we know in our hearts that we learn the greatest and most profound things by breathing, by seeing, by feeling, by falling in and out of love.

Douglas Coupland, *Life after God*

In returning and rest you shall be saved.

Isaiah 30.15

CONTENTS

ACKNOWLEDGEMENTS

For Joseph, Benjamin and Samuel,
with apologies for not always practising what I preach.

I dedicate this book to all those people who have helped me find joy and meaning in life: to my parents for giving me the firm foundation of sound loving; to my brothers and sister for their companionship; to Rebecca for the shared adventure of a lifetime; to my children for the many ways they have put me back in touch with wonder and delight; to the people I have ministered to as a priest and who have welcomed me into their lives at times of timorous joy and terrible sadness; to all those friends whose lives have inter-cut with mine. And through these relationships have come the little grace-filled moments that make up a lifetime: listening to my Mum playing Chopin, climbing Pen-y-Ghent, a quiet day at Bede House, riding bikes up the Camel Valley. I have received so much; and it is these moments and encounters more than anything – and the grace that is revealed in them – that has shaped this book.

I am also grateful for those who have read through the text and made many insightful suggestions. I read the whole thing out loud to Rebecca on a drive up to Shropshire and made lots of changes as a result. Kathryn Pritchard at Church House Publishing has been marvellous in keeping my nose to the grindstone, my eye on the ball and my ear attuned to the central purpose of this book: which is that out of patient attentiveness to the present an eternity can be grasped.

THE DIFFICULT BUSINESS OF STOPPING

> You have to allow a certain amount of time in which
> you are doing nothing in order to have things occur
> to you, to let your mind think.
>
> Mortimer Adler

Let us imagine the whole of this book as an exploration into the dynamics and possibilities of a single moment, an eternal now.

Or maybe that's too heavy.

Maybe I should just roll over and go back to sleep for an hour and dream a bit. Or go downstairs and make a cup of tea. Or run a nice hot bath and enjoy that delicious wastefulness of time when as the bath goes cold you gently release the plug with one foot and turn on the hot tap with the other, replenishing the water at the same time as it drains away. Oh, but what a waste. There are many people in the world today who won't get a glass of water, let alone an overflowing bathful. Really I should be more considerate. I should be getting on with something useful. And yet I have this feeling that all the really important things I've ever thought of have emerged from the well of this waiting, and apparently wasting time, which I discover is not really wasting time at all but using it differently. And I have this awful fear that one day I will no longer be able to lie in bed in the morning or wallow in the bath. I will have lost the ability. What a horrific thought; one to encourage a further burrowing down under the covers and a tightening of the duvet lest the grim efficiency of the world with its ticking clocks, busy schedules and insistent deadlines should overwhelm me.

But help is at hand, or at least a reminder that the world isn't as important as it likes to make out. One of my children is now a teenager. He sees life differently. Each day I marvel at his fantastic capacity to lie in bed. I moan about him – that is expected of parents – but really I am jealous. I observe the daring scope of his sloth with secret envy.

More worrying, I keep meeting other parents of teenage children who berate this astonishing capacity in their own offspring and say, rather priggishly, that they couldn't lie in like that even if they wanted to. But I could. For sure, the opportunities are severely limited – but left to my own devices, and without the clamours of work or having to attend to children, I'm sure I could still do it. I could lie in till lunchtime.

Now, I know that with age come changing patterns and require-ments for sleep. Many older people really can't sleep in even if they want to. But I am not thinking about this: not a physical condition that would prevent me, but some inner imperative driving me to conclude that it is wrong.

And yet, only yesterday morning, an opportunity for blissful nothingness emerged. I'm writing this at the end of the Christmas holidays and the children have not gone back to school yet. They had got themselves up and were watching television. My teenage son was still in bed (of course). And I lay in. I half slept and half woke and enjoyed for several hours that dreamy, in-betweeny state of living that hovers between consciousness and sleep. At about nine I got up, leaving my wife in bed, and made us both some tea. I took it back to bed and let it go cold. I dozed off for another half an hour. I slept a bit more, and I got up at about eleven. It was one of the best mornings I've had for ages. I don't want to do it every morning. But I do want to do it again, and in a little while I'll tell you why.

Now I could tell you the reason I lay in was that I have been so busy lately and working so hard that I had really earned it. But that's not quite true. I *have* been busy and I *have* been working hard, but I've also had most of last week off. In fact, it took me the best part of a week to de-tox myself from the busyness of life so that I had half a chance of arriving at a place of restful idleness at all. So I don't want to pretend that rest and play are only allowed as reward for effort. They are good in themselves. They lead us to places of self-discovery and renewed creativity.

We must confront the preening self-righteousness of those who claim they've lost the ability, because they either feel ashamed of admitting this secret pleasure or, worse, have genuinely arrived at the conclusion that lying in bed is somehow morally repugnant: an affront to the all-conquering work ethic of Western society which says we must be busy, busy, busy all the time. Shame, I can understand: none of us can avoid contamination from the frenzied roller coaster of the '24/7 work-all-the-hours-God-sends-you' culture we are part of. Even as I wrote the words 'got up at about eleven' I felt a twinge of guilt. Should I change that to ten? Is it a crime against the culture of busyness to admit such sloth? But that is what is being implied. Shame, guilt, busyness have won the day. You are only able to function on one setting: full-on busyness. Either that, or death. Is this why so many men expire as soon as they retire? They have never learnt to do nothing.

And so I look forward to the opportunities to lie in when they come along. I embrace them, wallow in them, push the guilt aside and luxuriate in the heavy moments of idleness. And I also start looking for other opportunities to stop and let the world pass me by. My teachers were right: I am a dreamer. It's just that the dreamer has been kept awake too long. The sleep deprivation of modern life has suffocated creativity.

When I was younger I can remember not just lying in bed, but lying on the sofa listening to music for hours on end; I can remember going for walks for no apparent reason and with no fixed destination in mind; just walking and thinking and idling away the hours. I can remember, as quite a small boy, lying beneath a huge chestnut tree and staring up into its branches, wondering at its nascent fruitfulness, and resting not just under its presence but somehow within it. All this is part of the person I am, but, for the present, it is chiefly lost to me. I am much too busy, and I have allowed busyness to invade my life so much that it gets harder and harder to be in touch with that other part of me which thrives on the creativity of indolent wastefulness.

But, when I do get back in touch, wonderful things happen. Not only do I become more myself – and that is joy enough – but from myself there comes fruitfulness.

And now I really must get up. Otherwise it will be as bad as yesterday and I'll still be in bed in the middle of the morning. I'm sure there are some important things I need to be getting on with. But let me just tell you about what happened in Dublin airport last year. It will explain a little more about the joyful art of doing nothing and where it can lead you.

I was speaking at a conference. I flew out from Heathrow and had a lovely couple of days with a wonderful group of clergy from the dioceses of Dublin and Glendalough. My return flight was due to leave at half past three. Or so I thought. I needed to check in at least an hour beforehand and as it turned out they got me to the airport at shortly after two.

However, when I looked at my ticket I discovered that my flight was not actually leaving until half past seven. Somehow I had misread or misremembered the time. I was too embarrassed to say this to my guests, so I bade them farewell and set about trying to get on an earlier flight. There was one available, but it involved paying a hefty surcharge. I could neither afford nor justify this expense so, instead, I settled down to a five-hour sojourn in Dublin airport. It is not a very big place, and after about an hour I had toured the shops, perused the newspaper and drunk a coffee. Still over four hours to go.

There was a restless impatience within me. I was cross with myself for not getting the time right. I was cross with the situation: so much time being wasted. The minutes ticked by with an aching slowness. The hours before me were an unwanted eternity. But then, imperceptibly, a calm came over me. The next four hours did not have to be a problem. They did not have to be a waste. Rather, they could be a gift. And as this thought settled in my mind I found I was able to just sit down and be still, and find contentment without having to be busy. I could relax and just be.

The busyness of the airport terminal carried on buzzing and humming around me. But now I was somehow in the crowd without being swallowed up by it.

I bought another coffee. I strolled around a bit more, but this time I was happy just to stroll and think and not worry about the time and what I was or wasn't going to do with it. After a couple of hours I got myself something to eat. And then I had a beer. And sitting in the bar I found my thoughts returning to some half-formed ideas for a poem that I had started musing on many years before. I got out my notebook (which I always carry with me – usually for worthy work reasons) and began to play with some ideas.

Slowly, a poem was born. Not a particularly good poem. Not a poem that I want to reproduce here. Not a poem that matters in itself. Neither does it matter that it was a poem at all. It could just as easily have been a picture, or even a doodle, or I could have got out my knitting. Or it could have been a snooze or a daydream. Or it might have been that in those moments of relaxed dreaming I would have remembered that I was a person who wrote poems/liked gardening/stripped down motorcycles or pressed wild flowers . . . delete as applicable, or add your own day-dreams.

What matters is what happened. Something was awoken within me while I was ostensibly doing nothing. I thought my flight was that evening, but actually the enforced delay took me on a much more exhilarating journey. Rooted to the spot I was able to travel back into myself: back into a part of me that had lain dormant for many years; crowded out with all the activity of work and busyness. For in the past I used to write a lot of poems. Just as many of us used to jog or crochet or swim or grow azaleas. And, although it is true that writing poetry (like many things) requires in equal parts discipline as well as desire, if there is no desire then no amount of discipline will ever get the poem written. Paradoxically, sitting in the airport lounge, I discovered that the discipline that was needed was the discipline of – well, here is the problem: what shall we call it? I want to use the word idleness, because that's what it feels like, but is even the use of that word allowing the culture that so abhors the vacuum of nothingness to set the agenda? When I speak about what happens when we do nothing I am not in any way wanting to exalt laziness. Rather, I want to celebrate what happens when we dare to stop and reconnect with a hiddenness inside ourselves where rest and play issue forth in all sorts of wild, unexpected and creative ways.

I am someone who has always found that writing poems helps me to make sense of myself and of the world of which I am a part. Therefore I believe I am a better person, or, rather, more the person I am meant to be, and better able to give and receive from others, when I write poems. But as this bit of me is lost and obscured by so much else that goes on in my life, when I don't write poems I am therefore *less* the person I am meant to be. This not only impinges upon my well-being but on the well-being of those around me, and ultimately on the well-being of everything. And the process of writing the poem in the airport lounge (whether the poem itself was any good or not) put me back in touch with this essential part of me, and therefore lifted my spirit and the spirits of those around me. So here I am, a year later, remembering those

7

happy hours in Dublin airport. And the reason I remember them so well is not only because what I experienced there was so real, so essential, but because it doesn't happen very often. My return to Heathrow was a return to the frantic treadmill of deadlines and demands.

Lest you think this book has parted company with reality before it has hardly begun, of course I realize that for the most part this is how our lives must be. We have our responsibilities and we must accept the demands they bring. It's just that the small boy who, when he should have been paying attention during maths class, was actually staring out of the window and dreaming, is still alive in me. And he wants to come out to play.

Here is the first of several gobsmackingly obvious and rarely examined conclusions that will be grappled with in this book: I have found that most of the really significant things I have learnt or thought or encountered in life have come from the well of this dreaming. And I am troubled for myself and for our world when every waking hour is filled with activity that sweeps dreams away and has no room for rest and play.

A recent survey announced the grim statistic that as well as working longer hours than they used to 30 years ago, people sleep, on average, two hours less per night. All the gizmos and gadgets that were supposed to have saved us time have only succeeded in raising expectations about how quickly people should respond and about how much more they should pack into each day. Whereas if you stop, and if you rest, and if you dream, all sorts of other things come to mind.

THE ABSOLUTE NECESSITY
OF BECOMING ECCENTRIC

You're only given a little spark of madness.
You mustn't lose it.

Robin Williams

So let me tell you about what happened the other day. I was shopping in town, probably being efficient and busy and rushing from one shop to another to get the things I needed, squeezing the shopping in between the other busy things I do, and taking no time to idle or gaze, when I passed a girl wearing a T-shirt on which was emblazoned the words: 'Galileo was wrong. I am the centre of the Universe!'

This pretty much stopped me dead in my tracks (a sermon illustration I thought!). Of course I'm sure the girl herself was enjoying the irony of the text, but at the same time its breathtaking conceit provides a penetrating insight into the human condition and the particular vanities of our present culture: a window on our self-centredness, for we do indeed imagine ourselves to be the centre.

We may have dispensed with God. We don't need that pathetic prop anymore. We may have stopped believing that politics can deliver progress, but we still crave something. Making sense of life, understanding cause and effect, asking the big questions of what life is about and why we are here, these things seem to be hot-wired into us. But now that all the big promises have fizzled out there is nothing left to do but reset the compass of the universe to self. I am the brightest star in the galaxy. And everything else revolves around me in dependent and adoring orbit.

Human beings have always been rather prone to thinking like this, but in our present situation it is more beguiling than ever. It's not that we no longer need or want other people (in fact we need and want them more than ever, for they provide the affirmation we crave), it's just that they don't exist in their own right as equal players in a drama whose centre is elsewhere, but as satellites upon which we can shine. The narrative that now makes sense of life, and around which other things revolve, is your life. Anything that happened before is of little value (for it was only a prelude to the real story which begins in us). Anything afterwards? Well, we don't think about this one, for the end of our life is truly the end of everything.

In order to bolster this conceit it becomes ever more necessary to disconnect with anything that might put us back in touch with the essential, independent 'otherness' of other things or other people. So you only care for other people in so far as these are people whose lives affect you, meaning that they are the ones upon whom you can shine, and from whom you can get what you need. And you stop caring about people whose lives are not in touch with your own, as if they don't exist at all. All the problems of the world, from teenage pregnancies to melting ice caps, AIDS, animal testing, third world debt, fair trade, race hatred and religious intolerance, are entirely inconsequential because they don't affect you. Hence there is little interest in the wider issues of justice and peace unless they directly impinge on our lives. 'I am not pregnant. The water levels are not rising in my town. I don't have AIDS. No one has ever harassed me because of my race or colour. No one has ever experimented on my pet cat, so why worry?' This is the attitude of self-love that we learn early.

Occasionally, one of these issues will affect us and we will set about changing the world on this one thing with a passionate intensity. But we fail to make the connection with all the other things that hold back the flourishing of the world. Politics, we say, like religion, has only caused the world's problems and can't solve anything.

But even as we say this, the foundation of our world view slips a bit. In order to keep ourselves at the centre, and in order to stave off the end of the universe (which is, of course, the end of our lives), much must be done to foster inner peace and outward beauty. And from the smorgasbord of New Age spiritualities, philosophies and self-help strategies a perfect creed of tranquil self-delusion is constructed, where crystals, herbs, incantations and a large dose of positive thinking dull the pain of impending self-demise. Creams and potions, designer labels, surgery, botox, collagen injections and harsh regimes of exercise and diet battle with the body's steady decay.

And even here it is possible to spot a hideous paradox in the culture itself. You are expected to put self at the centre and worship self-advancement, yet at the same time you are endlessly bombarded with images of how you ought to look and how your lifestyle ought to be. The only conclusion you can draw is that somehow being 'yourself' isn't good enough. It is impossible to switch on the television or open a magazine without seeing some youthful vision of sexually charged and highly toned humanity. With it comes the empty promise that this car, or that perfume, or this diet, or that surgical operation will deliver the body/salary/ sexual fulfilment you crave. And none of it does. Or, to be more accurate, it delivers just enough to get you hooked.

We wear the T-shirt, but its insistence that I am the centre of the universe now appears rather desperate; for the inner truth is that we don't feel this way at all. We pretend it is what we want, and we desire it with the same despairing hunger of any junkie, but in order to get it we now realize that what we really want is to be someone else. Our own pathetic imitation of humanity is too fat, too old, too ugly, too poor, too ordinary (too human, too frail). Actually, we hate ourselves. That is what believing yourself to be the centre has achieved. There is nothing at the centre except a self-loathing and a futile desperation to be someone else – someone rich, someone beautiful.

For this horrible malaise there is only one cure I know. It is to put something else at the centre. But how and where will we find such a thing?

For the time being let us put that to one side; the central message of this book is that stopping, and doing nothing very much in particular for a few hours, is a good thing to do, and that when you do it you very slowly start to rediscover yourself in relation to others and to the world itself. You value yourself but find your centre somewhere else. This does require a certain act of will: not just the stopping, but also the convincing that actually you are not the centre of everything; that other people really do exist; that they have the same feelings, anxieties, joys and heartbreaks that you do. It requires paying attention to others as well as yourself. And also resting for a little while; and even quietly observing other people and enjoying their presence without necessarily knowing who they are or having anything directly to do with them. This can be an enormous blessing. Try just sitting still in a crowded busy place and watching everyone around you going about their business and then fostering inside yourself a thankful spirit for the independence of all these people and your inter-dependence with them. They, with you, are all part of the vast and complex tapestry of human life and that itself is only a small, but brilliantly beautiful, part of a much grander scheme of immense loveliness.

And now we are halfway to another astonishing conclusion. This beautiful world of which we are a part spins on its axis and revolves around the sun without my help. The sun rose in the east this morning without my aid and will set in the west this evening whether I want it to or not. I do have an effect upon the world. Indeed, if we are to take an active interest in human flourishing and in the safeguarding of the delicate harmony of our planet, then little individual initiatives to save water, conserve energy, love our neighbour, will be of equal value as international treaties. It's just that in the very grand scheme of things people can best understand and appreciate their own position when they place themselves *off-centre* – having an influence, but also *being influenced*; acting and *being acted upon*: part of something bigger than themselves; part of something of which they are intricately and preciously a part, but which does not have them at the centre.

In other words – and to be precise – it requires an eccentric approach to life. For to be eccentric means, literally, to have your centre somewhere else.

In common parlance the eccentric is thought to be somewhat odd. This, too, is a fine thing to be; for if being sensible requires the slavish cycle of self-worship and self-loathing that we described, then being odd might be the best path to happiness.

THE EVEN TRICKIER BUSINESS OF KNOWING WHO YOU ARE

The real voyage of discovery consists not in seeking
new landscapes but in having new eyes.

Marcel Proust

So if you are not the centre of the universe, what is? Well, the best
advice I can offer is the same as in the first chapter: stop . . .
breathe deeply . . . if it helps, imagine yourself stranded for a few
hours in Dublin airport. Search deep inside yourself for those
memories and feelings that are most precious. These are the things
that can begin to put you back in touch with yourself and lead to
your true centre.

Now I know that not everyone will have these particular memories,
but can you remember the nervous passions and the trembling
delight of first love when the sound of your beloved's voice, or the
touch of their hand, could conjure joy, and when just seeing them
and being seen was rapture, and when the memory of presence or
the expectation of encounter set your pulse dancing? Or can you
just remember the aching thirst of loving and desiring someone,
even if that love was not returned?

Can you remember just being with someone who trusted you and believed in you and with whom you felt safe? It might be a lover or it might be a friend.

Or can you remember how it felt holding your first child in your hands for the first time? Or else watching your children as they sleep, running your fingers through their hair, wishing that time could stand still, wanting to hold this moment, and so many moments, for ever, into an eternity: thinking, who will be there to love them and hold them and stroke their foreheads on the last day of their life? Or, for that matter, seeing someone else's child; wondering at the exquisite mystery that you are here at all and that this particular new life began with that particular sperm and that particular egg and has now issued forth in this particular bundle of life? You don't have to be a parent to be amazed at the profligate beauty of a new human being. And all the scientific knowledge of how it came about won't take away the wonder, so that eminent gynaecologist and teenage mother alike call it a miracle.

Can you reach back into your own childhood? Can you remember what it felt like to be held tightly by arms and hands much bigger than your own? Have you known, and can you recall, what it is like to be cherished and valued just because you are?

But what if you have felt none of these things? What if you are reading these words and seething with anger and regret that for you childhood and love, friendship and parenthood, have brought as much frustration as delight? Or, worse, they have brought you neglect and abuse. Yet even the most neglected and the most appallingly abused carry within them the possibility of being loved and of loving in return. Indeed, this is what they long for. It is only this giving and receiving of love that offers them any hope. And the majority of people will have memories that they can return to, that define who they are and shape their lives; cherished moments when they knew themselves to be precious, moments that make life worth living, and cause them to rage against the inevitability of death. These moments are deeply physical – we tend to locate them in the stomach as much as the heart – but they are also what many people will call 'spiritual'. They seem to occupy a place in our consciousness where we are most truly ourselves (so much so that it floods our whole being). It is impossible to imagine what it is like for this not to be. And even when a broken and abused life has given us a meagre ration, these experiences are the ones we wish to build our lives upon, places within where love and passion, tenderness and delight inform and sustain us.

Although the world has many explanations for these feelings, the latest being offered by the decoding of the human gene, there is still a great resistance to being so unravelled. And this resistance is more than an anti-intellectual hankering over a simpler and more certain past, where people more readily believed and accepted a view of humanity that clearly identified these feelings and desires within something called the soul. It seems as if it is part of the DNA itself. Humans instinctively and intuitively believe there is something more to life than what they see around them. Human life adds up to more than the sum total of people's ability to explain themselves.

There is something in the centre – at the heart – that demands explanation. And people need an explanation that takes account of the spiritual reality that they still believe and experience to be the most important thing about themselves.

Surveys consistently show that most people in Britain still believe in God (though who or what God might be is not clear) and still pray regularly. Along with this goes a whole panoply of other beliefs and practices. Acknowledging that something is missing, people either start a spiritual search, or become beguiled and fascinated by spiritual things. Hence the growing interest in everything from horoscopes and yoga to pantheism, reincarnation, crystals and tarot cards. Far from being on the wane, we live in a culture where fascination with all things spiritual appears to be on the increase. And all this in a supposedly rational and scientific age.

Even if you are not one of those people who look for meaning and purpose in life through that growing pot-pourri of New Age spiritualities, and this is increasingly the case among the young, you have a spiritual dimension to life (even if you don't use the word) because you experience love and joy and sadness and, yes, even the darker experiences of greed and hatred. And if you are a spiritual seeker, then that is good: because there is a spiritual meaning to life and the pulse of this dimension can be felt in all things that are good and true. But, even if you are not, these things demand an explanation.

My explanation is simple: human beings are made in the image of God. This does not mean that God looks like us, but that the feelings and thoughts that are the foundation of our own understanding of ourselves have their origin in God. People, as it were, reflect back to God the consciousness and creativity out of which they are created.

As far as we are able to know, we are the only creatures in this universe who possess such consciousness. In fact the more cosmology reveals of the nature and origin of the universe, and of the place and origin of conscious life within it, the more extraordinary seem the coincidences that have come together to make this planet a fertile oasis within what may well be the barren emptiness of everything else. Of course, it isn't possible to know this, nor does it really matter for our purposes here whether there is conscious life in other parts of the universe or not, but it is interesting to note that the more that is discovered about the phenomenon of life that is us, the more we are amazed by our own fragile brilliance. We do not conclude there must be plenty more of it around: we are dumbfounded we exist at all. As Einstein observed: the most incomprehensible thing about the universe is that it is comprehensible!

Alone among the creatures of this world humans are able to live life beyond instinct. They are able to gauge and shape the life they have. They are able to reflect purposively on the life they lead. Their consciousness and desire to make sense of life have spawned a terrible creativity and have led them in directions that have been beautiful and appalling in equal measure.

But let me slow down a bit and unpack what this actually means, because there is something extraordinary about us humans that we have to try and account for, and we certainly need to celebrate. And this may lead us to the source and centre of our lives.

Human beings think and do incredible things. Look out of the window as your plane from Dublin airport takes to the sky and you will see a landscape fashioned and crafted by the needs and aspirations of human living. This is both extraordinarily beautiful and also, sometimes, self-centred and indulgent, for people abuse the environment upon which they depend, and lack respect for the natural resources they take too much for granted. But, nevertheless, it is astonishing. People harness the natural environment to support their dreams, and while we must learn how to do this in a way that will not damage the delicate equilibrium of our coexistence with other forms of life, I am optimistic – we are so fearsomely clever.

People build dams, skyscrapers, mobile phones. A neurosurgeon, in a feat of technical brilliance, is able to remove a tumour from the centre of the brain. Today's surgeons stand on the shoulders of so many hundreds before them in the trial and error of all human achievement. And all that goes to make these operations a success, from the video and computer technology, to the microscopic equipment, the fibre-optic lighting, the production of the kidney dish into which the clotted tissue of the tumour is placed, the collecting of the blood which someone somewhere donated and without which the operation could not take place; all this is a staggering tribute to the tenacity of human cleverness.

People ferment grapes into wine and blend different wines into fantastic vintages. They grind wheat into flour and from flour make bread. They learn how to preserve food with salt or vinegar. Or they harness the natural power of the atmosphere and make electricity, and then invent a thing called a fridge freezer. People travel around using the power of animals, and then make bikes, motorbikes, cars, aeroplanes to fly in, and then put a man on the moon.

All this knowledge grows and multiplies, is carefully communicated from one generation to another, and then built upon again. It used to be kept in books like this, and before that scrolls, and before that memorized and passed from person to person. Now it is available with a few clicks of your mouse. And the information that was once inside a library is stored on a memory stick you can keep on your key-ring.

And people do some other pretty amazing things, not because they are going to be useful or productive in feeding the world or advancing human knowledge, but just because they are compelled by something within them to create and understand and re-create and communicate the deep feelings of love, compassion and community that are inside them. People paint astonishingly beautiful pictures. They make sculptures. They write books. Some of us sit in airport lounges writing poems; others make scale models of Tower Bridge out of matches; and others float a giant Ferris wheel up the Thames enabling you to see London while gently and imperceptibly spinning round and round. Others devote a lifetime to improving their golf handicap. Some play darts in the pub. Someone somewhere knows the Latin names of all the moss and lichen, the wild flowers and grasses that are growing in the cracks in your front drive. And someone else worked out these names in the first place. Another person is the DIY expert who mixed the cement and laid the paving slabs.

Sometimes we run just because we feel like running, or we skip as we walk along. We hold hands with each other. We doodle on the telephone directory while making a call. We invent a whole new way of speaking to each other called text messaging – and we use it to send messages of love. We sing, we dance and we make music. And no one can say exactly what the music and the dancing mean, but we are still moved by it in incredible ways.

Sometimes the rhythm and the joy of a piece of music lifts you to your feet and you dance around the kitchen, or play air guitar with the broom, or mentally conduct the London Philharmonic while powering down the motorway. Sometimes you will hear a piece of music and it will reduce you to tears. Sometimes, just by its sheer beauty, a chord will be sounded deep within you, the language of the music beating in time with unfathomed, or deeply cherished, feelings inside. Or else a piece of music will evoke a moment from the past, transporting you back to a certain place and to certain feelings, and often to a certain person. Most of us have songs that we think of as 'our songs'. They connect to particular episodes, as if the whole of our life had a soundtrack to accompany it.

Even smell can do this. You can be walking down the street, not doing anything in particular (though, as I am at pains to point out, doing nothing in particular is a very good and creative thing) and suddenly a distinct smell will drift across your nostrils and you are taken back to a place and a special memory.

And people do incredible things for each other. They carve each other's names in the bark of trees. They write love poems. They play. They have bodies that can enjoy one another, and these exquisite pleasures are both creative and delightful.

As we consider human achievement, in all its vast, intricate and astonishing variety, we find our appreciation of ourselves expanded.

And each of us contributes to this in different ways, both in the things we enjoy and in the things we create.

For me it is the poems of Simon Armitage, Strauss's *Four Last Songs*, Louis Armstrong singing 'St James Infirmary Blues', Stanley Spencer's series of paintings entitled *Christ in the Wilderness*, Monet's *Water Lilies*, Rothko's expanses of colour, Mendelssohn's *Songs without Words*, and Bob Dylan's 'Blonde on Blonde'.

For you it might be the poetry of Shakespeare, Aretha Franklin, the Arctic Monkeys, the latest Harry Potter, or Beethoven's final string quartets. Or it might be the triumphs of modern medicine, or the wonders of the Internet; a Harley Davidson, an iPod, the thought of Jonny Wilkinson's drop goal when England won the Rugby World Cup in 2003, or even something simple that you use everyday, like a can opener or a corkscrew. All of these things are testimony to human ingenuity and creativity. We all find wonder in very particular, but wildly different, things. But they all have their source in our astonishing capacity to create.

But I also want to make the point that it is not just music in general that people like (or painting or architecture or sport). It is a *particular* piece of music, or a *particular* painting, a *particular* building, a *particular* golf course. It is in the precise distinctiveness that you experience joy. Therefore it is too bland and obvious to say, 'I love music'; rather I will say, 'I love that specific version of Willy Nelson singing "You are always on my mind"'. It never fails to make me cry. It makes me feel more human; and people all have their different and unique ways of sharing in this adorable abundance of delight.

At the same time we tremble in revulsion at the terrible things we do, our horrible capacity to abuse one another: the devastation wrought by the atomic bombs dropped at Hiroshima and Nagasaki, the methodical and carefully planned genocide of the death camps of Auschwitz and Belsen. Planes crashing into high-rise buildings. Or the race hatred and xenophobia, the greed and conquest, that got us to these horrors in the first place. Bullying in the playground. Or stealing a fiver out of someone's purse when their back is turned. A single word designed to hurt, and delivered like a precision bomb. Or else you look to the future, wondering what the genetic modification of plants, the production of human organs, the farming of embryos will mean for your children? And you can easily feel helpless.

Human beings are fiendishly clever, so terrible in their cleverness that it's easy to think that their appalling cruelty is sufficient evidence to dismiss the notion that they could be created by a loving God, let alone be made in God's image. But that is what I am suggesting. When you look into yourself, when you marvel at the love that is within you and acknowledge your terrible potential for good *and* evil, you catch an echo of the one who is the source of all life, and therefore your life.

To be made in the image of God is to be made in the image of the one who has made this universe, and has made it with a terrible freedom. And the universe possesses this terrible freedom because it has been made out of love. It is God who is the source and centre of our lives.

THE SCANDALOUS
HOSPITALITY OF GOD

> We're so used to standing on our heads that
> when God shows up, we think he's the one who's
> upside down.
>
> Robert Farrar Capon, *The Mystery of Christ*
> *. . . and why we don't get it*

You may feel it is a long way from lying in bed, or swanning around an airport lounge on a lazy afternoon, to believing in God, but bear with me. I cannot offer proof, but as Shakespeare observes in *A Midsummer Night's Dream*, 'imagination apprehends, more than cool reason ever comprehends'.

Most people have a frustration inside. They are too busy, too frantic, too driven. 'He wished he spent more time at the office' has not been carved onto anyone's tombstone! Or as best-selling life-management guru Stephen Covey observes: 'Many people spend their life climbing the ladder, only to discover it is leaning against the wrong wall!'

At the same time, there is a creativity that arises from leisure and restfulness. There is a hunger within us for meaning, and an unstoppable compulsion to try and explain and to create and re-create the world around us. And alongside this hunger a gnawing emptiness. When you find the time to stop and stare, you encounter an unaccountable 'something' that nothing else can quite explain.

What is this 'something'? What is the centre around which my life can flourish?

Let us suppose, for a moment, that it might be God and, travelling by way of the imagination, let us explore the possibility of God and consider how it might help us to make sense of ourselves and of our world. Let us suppose, if only for one of those moments that could be an eternity, that the energy and creative power that people experience in the inner stillness of resourceful repose has, as its source, an energy and creative power that is itself love. Even if you have no idea what the word 'God' refers to, let us use the word 'God' to describe the source of that love and creativity. And if it is God – if the word God and the idea of God are helpful ways of thinking about those things that are dearest and truest within you – then where else can this lead? How can you find out about this God? How can you test this way of making sense of life to see if it can help nurture and prosper the person you long to be?

First things first. The faintest trickle of water, burbling to the surface from underground sources deep within the earth, from which a mighty river takes its source: God is love. Not God is loving, but God is love itself. The Christian tradition – that set of beliefs and practices that flow from the person and teaching of Jesus Christ – begins with this astonishing claim. And whether you are particularly religious or not (and on the whole I feel that not being religious gives you a distinct advantage), it is important to remember that when people talk about love in relation to God they are still talking about the same thing – a real, fragile, tangible, self-giving love – the same love that they experience in their daily lives. It comes from a God who is this love.

You can also recognize that two of the hallmarks of genuine love are creativity and freedom. These are not religious ideas. Consider your own experience: when we are in love, that love is creative. We feel more fully ourselves when we are in relationship with one we love – whether in the blossoming of ourselves or else, more literally, in the wonderful creativity of reproduction.

Having a child is one most obvious sign of love's innate creativity. This helpless creativity, this desire for communion, to receive and to be received, is one of life's most beautiful and satisfying experiences. The Christian tradition says it is part of the nature of God. It says God can't do anything else. God's love, which is the source of all love, is always creative. In fact, when Christians speak about God, their most profound and inexplicable language concerns a description of God as a kind of community. God is known as Father, Son and Holy Spirit. This is a difficult notion even for most Christians to get hold of (and on the whole they try not to think about it too much), but hopefully it is sufficient to say here that within God himself (herself? Of course God is beyond gender) there is a giving and receiving of love. And once again, even if this is not your own experience; even if your being a parent or a child has only brought you bitterness, or, if experiencing childlessness, you have raged against the fertility you see everywhere else, love is still creative. It is creative in friendships. It is creative in the comfort others bring. It is creative in the kind and gentle words of strangers. It seeks to unite, and draws us into community with each other, and thus enables us to be more ourselves. We are not meant to be alone. Even in the darkest isolation, the rhythm of one human heart reaches out to beat in time with another.

The Da Vinci Code got a lot of attention for its speculation and conspiracy theory purporting that Jesus had married Mary Magdalene and sired a race – a holy blood line. The actual forgotten scoop of early Christianity is this belief in the community of God, a community where love is perfectly given and perfectly received and which is the heartbeat and the source of everything.

The Christian answer to the question of the origin of the universe is that the big bang with which the universe began – the tiniest hazelnut of matter expanding rapidly and creatively into all that is – was the simple consequence of creative loving.

When human cleverness split the atom it was discovered that matter transforms into expanding energy. When the universe was created, the beautiful energy of love overflowed into expanding matter. This moment, though it wasn't a moment because with the birth of matter came the birth of time, was an eternal, endless and immediate 'now' of pure loving that couldn't be anything but creative. And within this outpouring of created love was the cherished possibility (though not the certainty) that a creature could evolve and emerge that was able to return the love. Within the complex web of human relationships in all their many forms, we experience this to be true.

And love is free. It is given in absolute freedom. It looks for no reward other than the satisfaction of loving. It may hope for a reward and may long for love to be returned, but it cannot make this happen. It can only carry on being itself.

Scientists have sent probes deep into space to collect dust from the exhaust fumes of comets in order to observe the first moments of creation. Here is an extraordinary thought: you have done the same thing by sitting still and contemplating the full depths of a single moment. It is possible, within the eye of the imagination, to behold the creation of the universe.

You can do this by thinking about the false things you place at the centre and the great desire you have for rest and play, creativity and love. You can do this by considering the love that is inside you. Even if its shadow has overtaken you, and even if it has never had the opportunity to be expressed, you know it is there. And this is where you end up – alone with your thoughts, but totally upheld and surrounded by a myriad of hands and voices, joining you to a universe that is itself alive and whose every particle sings for joy. For I am supposing that the character of the universe is the character of unconditional – and therefore completely free – loving. This is also the character of humanity. Therefore I am supposing that human beings are made in the image of God. This is where your tremendous capacity to love and create comes from.

So whenever we experience love; whenever we clasp the hands of our beloved, feel the thrill of being welcomed home by a child or partner; or even feel the possibility of love, or of hope rising within us, or a glimmer of light challenging the too pervasive darkness of our own wrong choices; whenever we realize that there are some things we would die for (though they are more likely to be people than ideas), we are experiencing the echo of the creator God who made us out of this same substance (though it is not a substance): love.

Free and creative loving permeates our every cell. It is not just a secret pool within us that used to be called the soul, though it still feels this way and people will still use the language of heart and soul as the most ready way of defining what they feel. But it is more than this. It is part of our DNA, the fingerprint of the one who made us.

And if God is love, and if this love is the genuine article, then God delights in you just because you are. You are the beloved of God. That reciprocity of love that is inwardly given and received within the very life of God is extended out to you. You can be welcomed into God's community of love. God shares the thrill of your passions, your homecomings and your sacrifices. God weeps with you in your sadness; God cries out in dismay at your betrayals. God's heart is turned to you. And even if you lived all your life not knowing God and not returning this love, God would not love you any less. Such is the nature of love: it longs to be returned, but it will carry on loving whether it is returned or not.

If what I'm saying is true, then there is nothing you can do to stop God loving you, and nothing God will do to make you love him back. In this sense I am not suggesting that there is something missing in your life. I am not saying there is somehow a God- shaped hole inside you and you will always feel a little empty until it is filled. To put God at the centre is not to fill a gap. It is much more like resetting a compass. It is with God, and the knowledge of God at the centre of your life, that the joy and meaning and purpose that you have already found within yourself, can be redirected and multiplied, bringing greater joy and greater peace.

So, if all this is true, if there is a God who made and loves the world, why doesn't he make himself known? Why aren't God's purposes a little clearer? Why does all the evidence of dying and decaying seem to speak against this optimistic vision?

It is all very well to recognize the need to put something at the centre of life that is not merely self, and it is all very well to recognize the reality and durability of love, and even if the other explanations do not satisfy, if God really is the origin and the destiny of life – if God is to be put at the centre – shouldn't he communicate this with a little more clarity?

The Christian answer is he has! God has communicated his love and purpose with absolute clarity. But this was not an easy thing to do. God had to do it in a way that would communicate the fullness of love while safeguarding our freedom to choose how we respond. For if even a little of this freedom is taken away then the love itself becomes impossible.

There is only one way to do this: a way of painful and inevitable ambiguity, a way of fragile and self-emptying love. And so we turn to the strange story of Jesus of Nazareth and the incredible claims that Christians make about him.

THE POSSIBILITY OF A FREE LUNCH AFTER ALL

> Now – here is my secret: I tell it to you with an openness of heart that I doubt I shall ever achieve again, so I pray that you are in a quiet room as you hear these words. My secret is that I need God – that I am sick and can no longer make it alone. I need God to help me give, because I no longer seem to be capable of giving; to help me be kind, as I no longer seem capable of kindness; to help me love, as I seem beyond being able to love.
>
> Douglas Coupland, *Life after God*

I remember sitting in Wakefield Cathedral some years ago, idling away an hour while I was waiting for a service to begin. Well, I hardly need to tell you what wonders can unfold during such a time with nothing to do, but on this occasion I found myself being harangued by a man who was also killing time in the cathedral. He told me how vicious, fickle and hideous he considered God to be. He had some fairly cogent points to make and he made them with vim and vigour. There was no doubt about it: God was either a complete phoney or a total monster, and to believe in him was an act of vanity or madness.

When he had finished speaking I could only, as it were, raise my glass and say that I agreed with him entirely. In fact I went further and suggested that we toasted the demise of this ugly, vain God in whom I also disbelieved with equal fervour. He was not quite expecting this response from a Christian priest, but I persevered. Having danced on the grave of the false god we had rejected, I said that I would love to tell him about the God of Jesus in whom I did believe. This was a God who did not send the trials and sufferings of this world to test or punish us; a God who was not disinterested, immune or unaffected by the pain and tragedy we experience; a God who was not just concerned with whether we were good or bad, peevishly keeping some sort of heavenly log book and endlessly checking on our behaviour, only happy if we were forever abasing ourselves before him and begging for mercy, but a God who loved the world so much that he didn't come into it to condemn it, but to save it. A God who was involved in the joys and sorrows of the world; a God who knew what it was like to be human; a God who reached down to earth so that we could reach up to heaven; a God who made everything, and then graciously offered himself that we might share everything with him.

Now, he didn't become a Christian there and then. He didn't run from the cathedral singing 'Alleluia'; but he was both surprised and delighted, cheered and challenged, by a different way of looking at God – through the lens that is Jesus. Jesus is best understood as God's way of getting to know God.

There isn't time in this little book to say all that needs to be said about Jesus of Nazareth. But the basic point is this: when Christians talk about God they are talking about God as he is revealed in Jesus. Therefore, whatever anyone else says about God, Christians say that God became a human being, and that, in Jesus, God lived and died and shared a human life. This is an astonishing claim – so astonishing that even having read the book this far, you may at this point want to go off and do something far more sensible – that Jesus is completely God and completely human, that in his person heaven and earth meet together. He is not simply a brilliant public speaker, or a miracle worker, or a divinely inspired person, or even some sort of superman: he is God come down to earth.

Many people – like my good, and understandably angry, friend in Wakefield Cathedral – have never encountered God in this way. As a result, the whole idea of God never seemed to fit into the mess that the world was in and the crap that people had to live with every day. But if God shares all this, if he became a human being like us, it changes things. It doesn't make the suffering any less painful, but it does prevent us from supposing God is separate or immune from it all. It also tells us about God's longing. How else could God communicate his desire to enjoy communion with us, except by this way of coming among us?

God comes to us in Jesus to bring a new way of understanding and appreciating the whole of life. The life we already have is good and beautiful, but the uncomfortable challenge of the Christian faith is that only God can satisfy the deeper longings within us for joy and peace. Only God can properly be the centre of life. This is uncomfortable because even though many people recoil from it, reject it and ridicule it, it actually resonates with that aching hunger that the busyness of life just can't satisfy. And when we discover God at the centre (for God is already there waiting to be known) we discover lasting peace and lasting joy. Not a peace and joy we haven't already discovered in all the beautiful things of the world (for I have already spoken about the joyful mysteries of love encountered in all of life) but, experienced afresh, because God is the source of life.

Even if the love available in this world has let us down we can find in God a deep assurance that no matter what happens, in this life and beyond, in the darkest moments of doubt and despair (and even close to death) we are loved.

This is the great message of the Christian faith: that God loves us and that nothing can separate us from this love. You don't need to earn it. There is nothing you can do to stop it. There is nothing you need to do to receive it, save accept it as the free gift it is. And even if you don't accept it, or understand it, or hear about it, or if you reject it, it is still there waiting for you and you are loved just the same.

We will never be forced into acknowledging God. This is not supposed to be a hard sell. The offer is made, and whether we accept it or not, God goes on loving us. The greatest sign of this staggering truth is the death of Jesus on the cross. In an age when so many people know so little about the Christian faith, most people still know this: that at the end Jesus submitted to the most painful and cruel death. It is the ultimate sign of God's involvement with the world. God shares everything. God receives the worst rejection of all. Jesus comes to us with arms outstretched ready to embrace, and offering words of comfort and forgiveness to all who are prepared to listen. It is not God in the way religious people want God, or the way those who have rejected God tend to think of him, but this is the God you find in Jesus.

On the cross Jesus does away with all the rule-keeping, debt-collecting, point-scoring, merit-awarding rigmarole of religious systems that try to control God and limit heaven to people like us. The message that Jesus pours out on the cross with his own shed blood is that we are loved, accepted and forgiven. We are loved even if we don't feel very lovable and have never been loved before and don't even know what it feels like. We are accepted regardless of race, gender, caste, class, colour or creed. We are forgiven from all the things that marred, wounded and obscured God's image within us. We are even forgiven whether we are sorry or not, and whether we realize we have sinned or not, whether we even know the difference between right and wrong, or whether we believe sin exists.

This is what we chatted about in Wakefield Cathedral: a different way of looking at God; a way that is both ancient – because it is just the Christian story that has been told for 2,000 years – and new – because each of us needs to hear it for ourselves, and because sometimes the Christian Church seems to be too busy telling other stories.

The only question that matters is this: will we receive the gift? We must be able to choose whether to receive it or not, because otherwise it couldn't be love. We have a choice because we have freedom. And if we are not sure, or if it's never been commun-icated clearly, or even if we choose to reject it and carry on putting something else at the centre (usually ourselves), then the door is still open, the welcome mat is still out on the porch, the table laid, your place prepared, the ticket to the party is still valid: you just have to say the word and you're in.

There is one last beautiful twist of irony. Not only do we receive this as a free gift, but we are most likely to discover it, not by poring over sacred texts or working hard to discover some deep and secret wisdom that is impenetrable to all except those who earnestly search it out (the New Age lie – though I'm sure *The Da Vinci Code* will sell more copies than this, since for some strange reason illusion always seems to be more seductively exciting than truth), but by hanging around; idly pondering on our own experience; rejoicing in the love we have received and experienced; and then allowing a train of thought to open a chink in the armour of our agnostic world view, so we end up wondering: perhaps it might be true, this strange story, this religion that is not really a religion at all, but the joyful proclamation that all religion is finished with.

People don't need systems and rituals and programmes to find God and to be OK with God. They don't need to search for it. This wisdom from God is not the preserve of a spiritual elite. It's not that one religion is right and all the others wrong and you just have to make the right selection. All of it – all the longing of the human heart, the wisdom and beauty of every human tradition and every religious impulse within our God-created humanity – finds its fulfilment in Jesus, for he is the one through whom everything was made and he is made flesh among us so that we can know God.

This is the Christian claim that is the heartbeat at the centre of the universe: all the purposes of God as revealed in the life, death and resurrection of Jesus are best understood as a declaration of love delivered personally to each one of us. It is an invitation to live a new and abundant life. Either this is true, or the whole Christian edifice comes tumbling down. But if it is true, then it is the foundation, the centre, upon which everything else must be built. Everything changes. Contrary to all the sensible advice of an anxious and competitive world, there is such a thing as a free lunch. God himself has set the table and everyone is invited.

chapter 6

BECOMING THE PERSON YOU'RE MEANT TO BE

The fullness of joy is to behold God in everything.

Julian of Norwich

Some years ago I was taking an assembly in a school in Huddersfield and when I went into the staff room for a cup of coffee afterwards one of the teachers was bursting with excitement at what had happened in her classroom that morning. I never quite understood the educational purpose of the exercise, but what she had been doing was blindfolding the children one at a time and getting them to stand at the front of the class and identify various objects. One little girl – she would have been six or seven – came to the front. The teacher put on the blindfold and, to check it was on properly, asked her whether she could see. The little girl replied yes. So the teacher adjusted the blindfold and again asked her if she could see. Again, the little girl said yes. At this point the teacher knew something was up: the blindfold was definitely on properly; there was no way the little girl could see. So coming at the situation from a different angle the teacher asked the little girl: 'What can you see?' The little girl replied: 'Flowers, and trees, and rivers and mountains.'

It was so beautiful to think of this little girl standing there in the dark – and what could she see? Well, she could see everything!

Then I thought to myself: what will we teach this little girl? Well, we will teach her that she is wrong, that it's just her imagination, that those trees and flowers and rivers and mountains aren't real.

But of course, from the perspective of eternity, and from the wisdom shown us in Jesus, the little girl is right. She can see everything. In her stillness, standing in the dark, she is open to the entire created universe. The darkness is not dark to her. From within the darkness she receives the invitation to enjoy the light. In her mind's eye – or should I say her spirit's eye? – she sees the whole world.

What can we learn from this? And how can we emulate this attitude to life where each moment is a participation in every moment? First of all we must acknowledge again that God's eternity does break into our chronology and that we are children of God. This is the greatest fact about ourselves and it is one we need to acknowledge and live by if we are ever to find peace and joy. We are that part of this astonishing created order, which is able to look upon creation with the same delight and wonder that we find in God.

Human beings are like God. That is another amazing conclusion. We are like God in so far as we are capable of amazement. This is what is meant when we say that we are made in God's image.

But there are other ways that our lives mirror the life of God. First of all, people are social. Like God people are most fully themselves when they discover who they are in community with others. This happens in relationships, with friends, in family groups and in the communities in which we live, in both work and leisure. And Christians believe that God is a community of persons – the Father, Son and Holy Spirit.

Like God, you are distinct and individual. However you imagine God and whatever God is like, God is separate from the universe, distinct from the creation he has made. Each of us is also a separate creation. We are brand new. We all have a deep sense of self, a deep desire to make the best of life, and an inbuilt longing to find meaning, purpose and value for our lives.

Like God we are creative, wanting to love and receive love, to shape and understand our lives and environment, to better ourselves and to live life to the full.

But I am talking about real love, and not just dutiful obedience – our innate tendency to be individual, social and creative children of God can so easily turn in on itself. All too easily, people learn independence rather than interdependence, and become self-reliant and then self-seeking. They stop seeing the flowers and the mountains, and act as if things are only real if they affect them and if they can shape and possess them. People start to understand themselves not in relationship with others but over and against them. They build walls around themselves, their families, their communities, their nations.

It is said that the only human structure that can be seen from outer space is the Great Wall of China. How sad, that our most prominent mark on the universe should be our proclivity to protect and divide ourselves from each other.

The Christian faith calls this sin, and the first and most dangerous sin of all, the author of every other sin, is the enthroning of self and the denial of community. People exchange the fulfilment that life has to offer in community for a hedonistic pursuit of transient, self-centred and self-obsessed pleasure. It is the horror of this world view that fuels the malevolent gossip and casual bullying of so much of daily life. And then, one thing leading inexorably to another, the world is mired in the holocausts of ethnic cleansing, the pillaging of rainforests and the exploitation of the poor. Our world is infected by our own inability to live with ourselves. And if it doesn't affect us – no matter how much our self-obsessions have contributed to the problem – we don't care. This is the problem: people live as if no one else mattered. They cut themselves off from the concerns and needs of the world. They claim indifference, or immunity, or both.

And then something really hideous happens: we see the terrible things that are happening in the world and with a chilling superiority observe that we can't imagine what makes people behave in this way. 'These people are behaving like animals' we declare. Well, apart from the fact that very few animals act with the same greed and loathing as humans, the apparent innocence and implied moral superiority of this comment actually exposes the heart of the problem. By disconnecting ourselves from the outrages that others commit, and by reckoning them less than human, we pave the way for the next holocaust. Those who do the terrible things we see on our television screens are not animals. They are people like us.

The world today is not very comfortable with the concept of sin. We prefer to think that everything is relative and that there is a rational explanation for every one of our actions, however hideous and destructive they may be. But what if some of the wrong things we do or say are wilfully committed in the clear knowledge that they will do no good, except to ourselves? What if we do the things we know to be wrong and fail to do the things we know to be right? What if we make so many wrong choices that we end up being unable to distinguish between right and wrong; that we are so damaged and morally compromised that we are savage in our dealings with everything?

The deeper and less palatable truth about human beings is that as well as being capable of the most magnificent and selfless loving, they are also capable of the most appalling horror. And God doesn't stop us or control us. He will not intervene when we abuse and exploit and kill. He will not force our hands or hearts to love. Not because he doesn't care, and not because he is not able, but because that is the nature of love. If he intervened with our freedom in this way we would become incapable of love and therefore be less than human: just much-loved pets, not children and heirs. This does not mean he cannot help, but that he takes the terrible risk of letting people work it out. God shows people how they ought to live, but lets them choose whether to take notice or not.

So let's imagine that it is you who is wearing the blindfold. You are standing in the dark and having to choose what you see and how you live your life and how you respond to all that is around and within you. You need to make a choice. You need to decide whose side you're on. And in that brief moment of stillness, where you catch a glimpse of yourself as a child of God, and where the amazing wonders of the whole universe are revealed to you, you need to be open to the possibilities of forgiveness and redemption that are presented to you.

This requires an act of will. You can't just wait around, hoping that one day you will feel sufficiently penitent to say sorry, or morally determined to do right. It is a matter of acknowledging realities. When we are being really honest with ourselves we can acknowledge that we are not the people we want to be, let alone the people God wants us to be. All of us do still rake over the past, and often with good reason. There are things we have said and done that were damaging. People are hurt because of our words and actions. People are neglected because we neglected them. Good things are not done because we choose not to do them.

So the choice is real. Is the world random and meaningless, and the only viable option is to salvage what little pleasure you can while waiting for death to pull down the curtain? Or is there another way of living? And, if it is true that in Jesus we discover ourselves to be the beloved of God, the long-desired and inevitable object of creation; and if in Jesus an invitation is offered to us to discover the full abundance of life, by living in community with God and entering into the joy of God's eternal now, then we have to decide whether we are going to accept it or not. Then we have to re-orientate our lives around it.

This re-orientation will require three things: the first is gratitude. We just need to give thanks for the life that we have. We need to marvel more at the world, of which we are a part. We need to rejoice that in Jesus we can enjoy the company of God. All this is very good news.

The second thing is penitence. As we see life more clearly, and understand its purpose more intimately, we become more and more aware of how we have misused and abused the life we have. And whether we feel sorry or not – and sometimes it takes a long while to de-tox ourselves from the hedonism of our age to actually feel much penitence – we must humbly confess our need of God and our sorrow for the ways in which we have gone wrong. This can be done silently and privately at any time and in any place. It is painful, sobering and of astonishing comfort. Sometimes it is good to do it alongside a trusted Christian friend or pastor. Often it is done alone – though there is really no such thing as being alone.

And the third thing is living it – which is what the rest of this book is about.

PLUMBING THE DEPTHS
OF A SINGLE MOMENT

> Humans are the only animal able to feel the pain of
> sorrow that has been stretched out through linear
> time. Our curse as humans is that we are trapped in
> time – our curse is that we are forced to interpret
> life as a sequence of events – a story – and that
> when we can't figure out what our particular story
> is we feel lost somehow.
>
> Douglas Coupland, *Life after God*

Recently, Samuel, my youngest son, woke up in the night, filled
with fear and crying uncontrollably because he was scared of
dying. This is a dread that all of us have to live with. I remember
eavesdropping on a conversation some years ago: one person was
saying to another, 'How often do you think about dying?' 'Oh, not
often,' the other replied, 'only every couple of hours!'

Well, not all adults think about death that often. Many of us are in
permanent denial, pumping iron, and counting calories, and pretty
much hoping that with the right amount of exercise, a good diet
and a following wind we might live forever. Or else, when the cold
hand of fear grips our heart, we actually crawl deeper into
ourselves, staying with the fear and avoiding human company. But

Samuel came downstairs. He was looking for comfort and he was looking for answers. I heard his cries and met him halfway. We sat on the stairs, and I held him for a bit and asked him what the matter was. Between his sobs he told me plainly that he didn't want to die, and that he was scared of dying.

This is one of the hardest things about being a parent – trying to deal with those moments when your children realize their own mortality. Your natural instinct is to protect them from it, but you also know that part of growing up, and part of being human, is to face the knowledge of your own death. Your job, as parents, is to help them make sense of it.

But many human beings opt out of this altogether through complicated and insistent denial. Not just all that stuff we explored earlier, dreaming of a perfect body that will last forever, but more complex stuff, like having your body cryogenically frozen, ready for the day when human ingenuity will have found a way to thaw and resuscitate a corpse. By then, you will also be able to clone yourself a whole new body of choice. Won't that be convenient!

Or simple humdrum stuff, like just being busy all the time and hoping death might go away. It won't!

However fit or healthy you are and however successful your life and whatever the successes of medicine to prolong life, one day the end will come. It is waiting for us. A funeral director recently commented to me that he had buried a lot of very healthy corpses lately!

Other human beings choose religion. But it is a mistake to think they are all the same. Some religions teach of life beyond this one and how you get into it. At least this brings the dubious comfort of knowing who will and who won't get the tickets for eternal life. Other religions are for this life only. Whatever they offer it is for the here and now.

The Christian way – the way of Jesus – is rather different. The eternity of what lies beyond death intersects with the trajectory of time within which you live now. It is for now *and* for eternity. Like all the other good things being explored in this book it is part of the plumbed depths of a single moment.

So there we were – sitting on the stairs. And my son's crying and telling me he's scared of dying, and I'm wondering what to say in return and thinking how useless words can be when you want to express the things that really matter in life. So I held him tight, because, as you will see, being held tight by someone you love is the best way of demonstrating heaven.

As we held each other I told him that I got scared as well and that I didn't want to die either. I told him that I had some answers to his questions but that they weren't the sort of answers that really proved anything. I couldn't give him an answer to what happens when you die in the same way that I could tell him two and two makes four. But I could tell him what I believed and why I believed it, and why I based my life upon it.

So I told him I found comfort in the promises that God had made in Jesus. I told him what I've been telling you, that Jesus is God come down to earth, speaking to us in a language we can understand. By this, I don't just mean a spoken language, but the language of a human life. And I told him that Jesus was like a declaration of God's real wanting to be on our side. That God was finding out how it felt to be us, was reaching out to us. And that Jesus had told us and shown us that there was a life after this life.

He sobbed for a bit more and I sat him on my lap and dried his eyes. He then said to me: 'What's heaven like?'

Now, this is an interesting question, but one which I think is vital to answer in order to go deeper into the stillness of this exploration of attentive idleness. What *is* heaven like? Most people answer this question by thinking of a place, and then going on to imagine what it might be like and how you get there. I held Samuel in my arms and told him to think of heaven, not as a place but as a person.

Jesus does talk about going to a place and getting it ready for us, and then he says he will return and take us with him. When he says this I like to think of a great table laid and a place prepared for everyone at it. (It is the invitation to the party I spoke about earlier.) But the real assurance is not about the place itself, but about the fact that we will be with him. This is the great final promise: the life we have with God beyond this life is a life with Jesus.

And now I realize I told you all that stuff about Jesus in the last chapter without mentioning the resurrection. Perhaps I was worried that you would think me completely crazy if I told you that a man rose from the dead. But that is what the Christian faith declares. In fact, before anything else, the Christian faith is an announcement of this: Jesus who was crucified is risen. This is what the first followers of Jesus experienced, and everything they then went on to say or write about him was from the perspective of this event. His rising from the dead demonstrated that God was in him and with him in a way that was unique and in a way that added even more weight and significance to everything else he had ever done or said. Now, I know that I can't prove any of this to you, but I am persuaded that all the other explanations as to how the Christian Church came into existence seem even more fanciful when compared to this basic proclamation. How else would a bunch of uneducated and illiterate fishermen from Galilee have spread their strange message across the whole of the known world in such an astonishingly short period of time? And why else would they have preferred death to the denial of this message, unless they had experienced it to be true? They might have made the whole thing up. They might have been suffering from some sort of mass hallucination. They might have so wanted Jesus to be alive, and so felt his presence with them, that perhaps they convinced themselves of their own strange testimony. But actually these explanations don't fit the facts. There is evidence from archaeology and ancient history of the rapid spread of the Christian faith. There are accounts of the bravery and gracious humility with which the first Christians refused to deny what they had experienced, and many were killed because of it. Would you spend your life sharing with the world something you had fabricated? Would you die for something that you only thought might be true?

As with everything else in this book, you will have to decide for yourself what you make of it, but if it is true, if Jesus in his life and death was God come down to earth, and in his resurrection was earth taken up to heaven, then whatever else heaven might be, this is something you can be sure of: to be in heaven is to be with Jesus. And to be with Jesus is to be with one in whom you can be completely yourself. It is to be with someone who knows you better than you know yourself, someone who knows what it is like to be human. He sees you as you truly are and he still loves you. He sees what you can be. He is on your side rooting for you.

To be with God in this way is like being with a dear friend, a child, or a lover, someone with whom it is sheer delight just to rest in contented silence. We feel more ourselves, and more at peace, when we are with this person. Somehow, to be away from the person we love is also to be away from ourselves. In the embrace of love we don't just find security and peace, we find our true selves. And if you have not had this experience, if life has let you down in this way, then it is an experience that is open to you. It is possible, with God, to find security and acceptance, to be received in love.

This is what heaven is like; being with a person who not only makes you feel good about yourself, but who does this by acceptance, love and forgiveness so you end up more yourself than you were before. This is what happens when God is at the centre of life.

And, of course, the best way of exploring this isn't to try and explain it, but to think of those moments in your own life where you have been in the presence and loving embrace of someone you love. If you have never had this sort of experience then it does become harder to imagine the love of God. There is no point in pretending. If family and friends have let you down then it's much harder to trust anyone, let alone God. But it doesn't mean that the love and acceptance is any less real, or any less available. In God's presence you can be accepted and loved and enabled to become yourself. For some people this will require a much greater risk. The experience of being let down in the past makes it so much harder to be vulnerable and risk getting hurt again. This is why the Christian Church needs to work much harder at becoming a place of open acceptance, especially for those who have been worn down by the confusions and deprivations of life. Christian people need to model for the world the welcome that is offered by God.

But when you can remember being held tight by a parent, or think of being in the presence of a trusted friend, or you recall a beautiful moment of intimacy – perhaps those moments after you have made love, when physically elated you rest in the company of the one with whom you have conjured such delight, and just being with them, resting with them, is bliss and comfort – you are experiencing a foretaste of heaven. And if this is true, if heaven is to be with Jesus in this kind of exchange of love (which is also to be taken into the very life of God), then we can't just talk about heaven as a place we go to when we die: heaven is now, a present reality as much as a future hope. Indeed, time itself begins to be experienced differently. It still exists as the unavoidable frame in which our lives on earth are lived, but within it we experience another dimension of being, the dimension of eternity. The 'forever' within which God dwells claims a foothold in your heart.

When Jesus said that he was leaving, that he would prepare a place for his friends and then return and take them with him, the New Testament records that one of the disciples listening was Thomas. Known as Doubting Thomas he often provides a helpful, questioning counterpoint to the drama of the story. He asks an all too human question: 'We don't know where you are going, so how can we know the way?'

For the first disciples the thought of Jesus' leaving, and at this point in the story the dreadful possibility of his dying, was like having their centre ripped out. For us, the thought of our own dying, the contemplation of our own annihilation and the end of everything that seems certain, fills even the most faithful believer with fear. But Jesus' reply to Thomas is of huge relevance. He says, 'I am the way, I am the truth, I am the life, no one can come to the Father except through me.' Sometimes Christians have used this text for an inappropriate triumphalism in their attitudes towards other religions. But for our purposes we can simply see that Jesus means that the way to life, the truth about life, and even life itself, are focused in him. This is an even more staggeringly outrageous claim than the ones I have made already. All the common sense logic and sophisticated wisdom of the world rails against it. Indeed, there is only one possible justification for such a preposterous claim: it is true. And this is the Christian belief – that the way, the truth and the life of God are focused in Jesus and that you can enjoy life with him and that this life can be found and experienced here and now. In this sense heaven is already among us: not a place to be found, but a new reality within which you can dwell, so that each passing moment ceases to be a moment lost, another moment closer to the grim finality of death, but a theophany (which is the posh theological word for a revelation of God). This is what people mean when they talk about 'living the Christian life'. It doesn't mean the fear goes away, but that you live with a certain attitude to time, and with a delight in, and an attentiveness to, each moment and all that is contained in it: for each passing moment is a participation in eternity.

chapter 8

LEARNING TO FEEL AT HOME

> I find myself increasingly happy contemplating simple things now I am in the springtime of my senility.
>
> Richard Chartres, Bishop of London,
> *Church Times*, 24 February 2006

I've told this story elsewhere but I must tell you again about what happened to me some years ago when the council came to tarmac the pavement outside our house. It's one of those experiences I keep returning to and talking about because it was for me a moment of revelation. A couple of days after they had finished I came out of the house and was walking along the pavement when I was stopped dead in my tracks by a tiny sliver of green. It was really the smallest speck of something or other, I don't know what, but definitely a plant clinging to the tarmacadam and forcing its minuscule roots into whatever moisture and goodness had already collected in a cavity so small and so unlikely that you wouldn't have thought that life could prosper there at all. And it had only taken 48 hours. Only two days after the tarmac had been laid and nature's expeditionary force was already on the march, reoccupying its territory! As I stared in astonishment at the tenacious creativity of this little speck of life I was overcome with a huge desire to get down on my knees, there and then in the street, and praise God. It just seemed so incredible. I felt connected with the wild, mysterious and insistent creativity that is unstoppable in our world; this astonishing oasis of life. Pick up a stone and there is a colony of woodlice underneath. Forget to clean your mug and a film of bacteria forms in a few days. Leave your tarmac untended and soon a forest will have grown. I stared in wonder, and I longed to praise God.

But I didn't get down on my knees in the street. That's the real reason I'm telling you the story: it's not that I didn't feel the wonder of creation, it's that I couldn't seem to do anything about it. I had this overwhelming desire to praise God, but I remained underwhelmed. I probably thought I would look stupid if I got down on my knees in the street. I was worried what other people might think or say. Yet, as I tell you this story, there is another bit of me that is profoundly embarrassed. Why is it, that in those rare moments when God seems so real, and when I do experience the joy of God's eternity and boundless creativity, I can't enter into it? Why is it that I keep it at arm's length, more concerned with its potential as a sermon illustration (or something to write about in a book!) than simply enjoying the moment?

At this point I need to introduce another key saying of Jesus: 'If you want to enter the kingdom of God you must become as a child' (cf. Matthew 18.3). These are radical words, but they are often misunderstood. Jesus doesn't just mean you must have childlike trust in God, which is the usual spin; he means enter into and receive life as a child. For children have the great ability to receive life as a gift. They are able to enjoy life. They will have no problem delighting in the scraps of life that spring up in the tarmac. While you are busy doing important adult things, they will be dancing in the shafts of sunlight that you barely even notice. They are at ease with play. Their minds are fine-tuned to wonder. I don't wish to get overly sentimental about children (I've got three so I do know what they're like!), but the important distinction seems to be this: children have an incredible ability to dwell completely in the present moment. While I spend so much of my life raking over the past or fretting about the future they are at home in the here and now.

And once again we need to slow down a little. What does that last sentence mean? Isn't it the case that so often we are thinking about what has gone before us? Dwelling on missed opportunities, replaying conversations in our heads, bearing grudges against those who've offended us, wishing we had made different choices, fantasizing that life could be rewound and we could do things differently. Or else we are busy planning our next move. Worrying about what tomorrow holds, dreaming about promotions, pay increases, summer holidays and sexual conquests. But what we are not doing – what can be seen in small children – is dwelling in the present moment. When it comes to the present, we're not present!

Well, another wonderful common-sense by-product of thinking of time as a participation in, and a preparation for, eternity is that we are enabled to be reconciled to the past. What has happened has happened. It cannot be reclaimed or relived. We need to understand the past (and often say sorry for the ways we have abused or misused it) but we also need to move on from it. And it is not that we should stop caring or preparing for the future, but not as a way of avoiding what lies before us. Whatever you feel about God, and whatever you feel about heaven, there is one thing everyone can agree on, and it is that this little moment now is all we've got for sure. As you read these words, and as I write them, we are dwelling in different moments in the chain of time that began when the universe was created and that will conclude when the universe ends. This is the time we have, and this actual moment now – you reading, me writing – is the only thing we possess with any certainty. But at the same time (or in a different sort of time that breaks into the same time) we have been dwelling, from the beginning of the book, in another sort of time, a kind of 'plumbing the depths of a single moment' sort of time, and reintroducing ourselves to life as a series of wonder-filled moments. It was in such wonder-filled moments that I found I could write a poem; that I was able to stop and contemplate the wonders of the love that is inside me, and could imagine that this creative force of love connected me with the source and origin of the universe; that I could stop and think about the person of Jesus, not as a great teacher, but as the one who channelled and communicated the love of God. It was in such a wonder-filled moment – smiling and dreaming – that I was able, at last, to accept life, not as a problem to be solved, but as a gift to be enjoyed.

It isn't easy to do this. I declined the opportunity to kneel in the street and give thanks to God for a little speck of something that was growing in the pavement. But it was still one of those wonder-filled moments that bore the invitation for community with God. But while our world still values busyness and productivity so much, people are always going to be tempted into thinking that the only way of finding meaning in life is to be busy and productive. But now and again, when stillness and solitude are forced upon us (like in Dublin airport), we glimpse it. Then we find stillness filled with eternity, and solitude a gateway into the community of God. But for the most part this doesn't happen. We are too embarrassed. Or else we would rather talk about it, or write about it, or do anything other than stop and enjoy it. Or we're just too busy. There isn't time, we say. But saying this is to sell out to the idea that time can only be experienced as a finite supply of minutes and years.

Take a deep breath. Put this book down for a minute and stare out the window. Enjoy what you see. Whatever it is, see it and value it as the precious gift of the created universe presented to you in this gracious moment.

OK, are you ready for it?

Time can also be the eternity of a single moment. And time on earth could be lived as one eternal moment after another, until, beyond death, we enter into the eternal now of God's eternal presence. To experience time in this way is a taste of heaven. It is an invitation to live life differently. It might also be the best way of living life joyfully, whether you believe in heaven or not. And it could also be the best way of finding out whether heaven exists.

Such a way of experiencing time brings the possibility of new delight and new joy in the people and things around us. It offers the possibility of opening yourself up to amazement, and for finding that the inner slob within you is really the little child you must become if you are to enter God's kingdom. So that on your deathbed you are not grasping for a few more moments, pleading with God for a reprieve, or angry with medicine for its failure to deliver immortality; rather you are at peace, dwelling in the final moment of chronological life, and welcoming the 'eternal now' it has been leading to.

When people say they are children of God, this is what they mean: living and enjoying life as a child in readiness for heaven, experiencing heaven now.

chapter 9

A BEGINNER'S GUIDE TO SITTING STILL

> People go abroad to wonder at the heights of mountains, at the huge waves of the sea, at the long courses of rivers, at the vast compass of the ocean, at the circular motion of the stars, and they pass by themselves without wondering.
>
> St Augustine

A couple of years ago I was due to lead an assembly at a Church of England comprehensive school that I visited regularly. This is a tough gig: seven or eight hundred adolescents, crowded into a hall first thing on a Monday morning, and forced to endure a hymn, a prayer, a worthy talk and, usually, a ticking off. One rises to give the talk to be greeted by a sea of faces grimacing back, as if to say, 'Go on then: impress me!'

On this occasion my anxiety levels were particularly high since I had not really prepared anything much to say. It was the beginning of Lent, and I had a vague idea about encouraging them to take something on rather than give something up, but as I walked to the school I was all too aware that I was in the fast lane of the motorway, with no petrol in the tank and I had just driven past the services!

But these moments of panic can also be moments of prayer, moments when we are more open to the wiles of God. And it was almost as I got up to speak that a crazy idea was suddenly born within me. Now, I don't really know where these ideas come from. They appear to come from without and so it's hard to even categorize them as your idea at all. It is like a gift. Suddenly one is aware of what to say and what to do, and if there was time to analyse it, or even prepare it more carefully, it wouldn't have the same power. So I stood up and found myself saying something like this:

> We live in a crazy, frantic world. Our world is full of movement and noise. Even this morning in the few hours since you woke up you have probably filled your time with the radio, the TV, the computer, the play-station; you've probably phoned someone and texted half a dozen others. As you got dressed, washed, showered, ate your breakfast, came to school, noise and busyness have been accompanying your every move. I believe many of the world's problems are caused by our inability to sit still and to be quiet and to reflect. I believe that in this season of Lent we should try to give up being so frantic, and we should take on some moments of stillness.

Then I stopped, as if I had lost my thread (actually it felt as if the thread were being handed to me inch by inch, and even I was not aware what was at the end). And I said to them, 'Hey, you don't know what on earth I'm talking about, so let me give you a demonstration. Let me show you what I mean. This is what I'm suggesting that you do, each day in Lent, for exactly one minute. It will change your life.'

I then picked up a chair, placed it in the centre of the stage, and slowly and carefully sat down upon it, with my feet slightly part, and with my back straight and with my hands resting gently on my knees. And for a minute I sat still. I didn't say anything, and I didn't do anything. I wasn't even consciously praying. I was just sitting there. And I breathed deeply, and I thought about my breathing. And when I reckoned the minute was over, I stood up.

But before I could say my next bit there was a huge, spontaneous round of applause. Now, I had done lots of assemblies in that school. On many occasions I had slaved over what I would do or say to capture the imaginations of the young people. But I had never had a response like this. In fact, in the days that followed, I was stopped in the street on several occasions by parents who told me that their child had come home and told them about the priest who took assembly and just sat on the stage in silence for a minute and then suggested they might do the same thing. Because when the applause died down, that's what I said. I just suggested that sitting still, being silently attentive to things deep within ourselves and things beyond ourselves, would make a difference. You didn't need to call it prayer. You didn't need to call it anything, because it would be in these moments of sedulous stillness that God could be discovered.

Like all the best sermons, I really needed to hear that one myself. I shudder to think of people who know me reading this book. I fall a long way short of the diligent day-dreaming I am recommending here, and they know it! But I believe that people will either recover this way of living and enjoying life, or they will perish. We urgently need to stop imagining everything is so urgent. Thus we will learn to nurture our inner slob.

So here is a practical way forward:

Get a chair. Not too comfy, not too hard; a dining-room chair will do. Place it somewhere quiet and peaceful. You may even wish to place it in a window so that you can look out, or have some other pleasing things to look at around you – some flowers, a candle, a picture of something lovely. But don't worry too much about this: soon you will be closing your eyes.

Now sit on the chair. Shuffle around a bit on your bottom and you will discover that at the base of your spine there is a bone for sitting on, and if you don't slouch, and if you get yourself onto it properly, then your back will be straight and you will be sitting upright and comfortable.

Now position your legs. Don't stretch them out or cross them, but sit with your feet slightly apart and then rest your hands upon your legs, just above the knee. Try to have your neck straight and look straight ahead.

Now breathe carefully and deeply.

Think about your breathing. Concentrate on it and don't think about anything else for a few moments.

Feel the air being drawn into your lungs and allow your chest to swell with the air that you are receiving. And when your lungs are full – and fill them much more deeply than you usually do – hold it for a moment, and don't yet breathe out. Enjoy the sensation of your lungs gorged on air and your body still. Be attentive to this most basic function of your body – the in and out of your breathing. And then exhale the air slowly. Almost blow it out.

Then breathe again, and as you breathe in think about all the good things that you long to take into your life; all the things that you are thankful for. Maybe even count your blessings on each of your inward breaths.

As you hold the air in your lungs, be thankful for the gift of life itself. Become aware of your dependence upon the air around you and upon the taken-for-granted motions of your body.

Breathe out again, this time expelling from yourself all thoughts of irritation, bitterness, frustration and regret. Rid yourself of the anxious, hectoring desire to be important and to be at the centre. Allow yourself to be part of the creation, dependent upon the resources that come to you as a gift from outside yourself.

Then, still conscious of your breathing, but not thinking about it so much, close your eyes and allow the deep rhythm of your breathing to still your whole being. Hold the stillness and, without particularly trying, experience a greater openness to everything that is around you. At this point you may wish to turn your hands over, so that your palms are facing upwards. The slight vulnerability of this action will increase that sense of openness, and express a desire to receive.

Now you are still. You are centred. You are beginning to pray. But it doesn't much matter whether you call it prayer. It is a way of being still in the midst of busyness.

I have practised sitting still like this for many years and sometimes I have been able to remain motionless and attentive for as long as five minutes, but it is usually less. Other, far more centred people than me can sit still for hours. But it is not the length of time that matters; rather it is a case of nurturing a certain attitude to life and developing an increased desire for silence and for attentiveness.

It can be practised anywhere: at home in a quiet moment, or on the train, or on a park bench. But it is my fervent belief that if everyone learned to sit still like this the world would be a much happier place.

And if this sitting still seems like too much too soon for a busy person like you, then seize the opportunities that daily life offers. When the sun is shining and there are five minutes to spare, lie down in the sun. Enjoy the feeling of the heat on your skin. If you are a commuter, then from the hours you spend on the train each day, turn a few minutes into moments of contemplation. If you go for a walk, then make sure there is also a moment to stop. And if the kids will let you, lie in bed a bit longer this Saturday!

SLOWING DOWN, SHUTTING UP AND SPEAKING OUT

> A piece of cheese, a bottle of beer, and a twenty-minute nap would solve more of the problems of industry, politics and the church than all the pretentious martini-logged luncheon meetings in the world.
>
> Robert Farrar Capon, *The Supper of the Lamb: A culinary reflection*

Modern life is crowded and cacophonous. Everywhere you turn there are more people shouting at you, demanding attention and wanting to consume your time. Drastic action is needed. So chuck out the instant coffee. It's not just that it tastes horrible; I want back the time it robbed me of. The superficial attraction of its speed didn't save me time; it just encouraged me to cram more in. What people need in their lives are things to slow them down. Labour-creating devices and time-wasting strategies are what I'm after. They will generate opportunities for stillness and reflection. So, here are some crazy things to consider.

Don't make tea by dunking a tea bag in a mug. Buy some proper tea. And warm the pot. Spoon in the tea carefully and let it mash. Observe the little rituals that used to be commonplace and that reward you with two or three minutes of having to wait. In fact, try not to buy any instant anything. It usually tastes ghastly anyway. Instead choose the things that take time: real tea and real coffee made in a way that requires effort and attention to detail, and which forces you to pause, to wait, and also to appreciate, to care.

Throw away that electric razor which allows you to shave on the hoof, and buy an old-fashioned shaving brush, some shaving cream and a razor blade and do it that way.

Buy a bike.

Keep to the speed limit.

Walk the dog a bit more.

Start learning the names of the flowers in the hedgerow.

Grow some vegetables. You only need a tiny little plot of land, even a window box will do, to get back in touch with the most wondrous giftedness of creation. Yesterday my son and I planted sunflowers and carrots, radishes, runner beans and pumpkins, and all on a bit of earth only ten feet by three.

Don't use a hose to water them; not just because there is probably a hosepipe ban in place, but because walking to the tap and filling up the watering can are excellent things to do.

In fact, why not buy a water butt and start appreciating the rain a bit more when it falls?

When you start opening up your mind to the little rituals that can be restored to life you are given back the precious gift of waiting and pondering.

Bake your own bread, or at least cook a few more proper meals and don't rely so much on the gruesome pap of pre-packaged food.

Or even better, cook a risotto; it is quite the most time-consuming recipe I can think of. You have to stand at the stove stirring all the time as vast quantities of wine and stock are absorbed by the rice. But as you stand there, irritated at first that it is all taking so long, and impatient to be finished, you suddenly find that the time that seemed to be consumed is actually being given back to you as a gift. You have the gift of time to just stand and stir and ruminate and dream. And if it is a big risotto – like the one I made last night with my eldest son and my mother who was staying – then there is room for more than one wooden spoon, and you can all stand there stirring and talking and enjoying a God-given space in the day.

So never speak of wasting time or spending time. Rather, say you are enjoying it or giving it freely away.

Never say you have an hour to kill. Rather, say you have an hour to revive, to bring to life, to ravish.

Watch the television a bit less and enjoy what you do watch a bit more.

Get round to writing that novel. Or at the very least write that letter – and yes I do mean letter, not email.

Of all the things that were supposed to save us time, but actually ended up demanding that we fit more things into the same finite number of hours available, surely email has the most to answer for. Not only does it demand attention, expecting me to do more and more, it robs me of time to reflect. It always wants an instantaneous response. It has not given me more time; it has filled my finite time with more things.

So, do not be a slave to the computer. Be disciplined about when it is switched on and when it is switched off. Just because broadband makes it possible, you don't have to be available all the time. That email which is shouting at you for a response today can probably wait till tomorrow. Instead of replying go and make a cup of tea. The considered reply will be better anyway.

And why don't all of us make a pledge to think a bit more carefully before sending any emails? We can be sure that most of the ones we will send today would never be sent at all if the communication still cost us a stamp. So who do we think we're kidding? This is not communication at all; often it is just ranting, getting things off your chest, chatter, attention-seeking, copying everyone in on some half-thought memo that didn't really need to be sent in the first place.

Right; now I've got that off my chest, back to some more positive things to do. As well as learning how to slow down most of us also need to learn how to shut up.

Well, see what I've written about emails above ... but generally we live in a very raucous world. It is as if we have become addicted to noise. The radio or the television constantly chatters in the background. Many of us have televisions on simultaneously in several different rooms. While one person is watching one television someone else is watching another, or fiddling around on the computer. Or playing on the X Box. Or listening to their MP3 Player. And so it goes on. It is as if we are frightened of silence.

We need to recover the beauty of solitude that can be found when the noise fades away. We can do this either by literally switching everything off for a while, or by developing an inner sense of stillness that enables us to stay calm and quiet while the noise carries on around us. This is where practising the fine art of sitting still will help enormously.

But we should also think about our contribution to the noise. Are you someone who has forgotten how to be still? Are you someone who always has to say something? When you are with other people are you really listening to them, or are you clamouring impatiently to get your word in?

There are few things more affirming than knowing you have been listened to. By practising the art of listening to yourself and developing an openness to things around you, you will also find that you are better able to listen and attend to other people. You may even find that you are able to love them. You will be more aware of your connectedness. You will not always be rushing to say things yourself. You will value the ideas and contributions of others.

So here are a few practical things to do to make sure there is some silence in your life:

Prune your collection of televisions.

If you are able, have at least one room in your home that is free from televisions, computers or even radios. Or have a happy hour when they are all switched off.

Make sure there are at least a few minutes each day when you are dwelling in complete silence.

In conversation don't always feel you have to be the first person to speak.

Take a day off and go and stay with a religious community and enjoy a day of almost total quiet.

Paradoxically, the noisy world is also an astonishingly lonely world – lots of chatter but no conversation; surrounded by people, but without community. Many of us start the day alone. More than ever before, people live alone. We travel to work alone. We pass through an automated ticket barrier onto a conductor-less train. We arrive at work and swipe ourselves in. We skip lunch and buy a sandwich from the supermarket, tapping in our PIN to a checkout assistant we don't even look at, let alone speak to. Or perhaps even the checkout is automated now. Many of us eat alone. Conversations and business dealings are tapped on to the keyboard of a computer. We go home to watch television alone and reacquaint ourselves with the community of Albert Square. But we don't even know our own next-door neighbour's name.

It's quite easy nowadays to go through a whole day with virtually no real face-to-face contact with another human being. Our reliance on technology enables – even encourages us – to avoid human contact. So much so that if someone does strike up a conversation in the street or on a train we look at them with deep suspicion.

When I was a little boy – at my primary school having to wear a cap as part of my uniform – my mother instructed me to raise it at any adult I passed in the street and say 'Good morning'. I have to say this little discipline of love has never left me. I don't quite start up conversations on the train – well, not often – but when I'm out walking the dog I will greet the people I pass by. Only this morning a woman who was also out dog walking looked at me in dazed horror as I said 'Good morning', and quickly averted her gaze.

What has happened to us? How is it that we have become so isolated from each other, so terrified of our neighbour? We have successfully betrayed that foundational belief that we belong to each other as part of a common humanity. And once that cornerstone is ripped away the rest quickly crumbles. Our whole edifice of ethics and community is built upon the recognition that I am my brother's keeper; that people do belong to each other; that there is such a thing as a common humanity and a common good, and for the Christian, to live like this is also to know that when you offer acts of service and kindness to each other you are offering them to Christ himself.

Only a deep appreciation of each other that flows from our indwelling in the present moment can begin to save us. Yes, we must know when to shut up, but we must also practise the gentle discipline of speaking out; of initiating conversation, of remembering all the very good reasons why our parents taught us to say 'please' and 'thank you'. These good manners oil the wheels of civilized living, subtly changing the way people look at each other, and opening doors of opportunity for others to stop and acknowledge the reality of what is before them. But this can only happen if we ourselves are seeking to nurture that stillness out of which such appreciation flourishes.

This sort of speaking out has another positive impact. By learning to value others, and by honouring their individual createdness and inter-connectedness with us, we discover a passionate concern for justice. We start to really care about the inequalities and injustices that corrupt our world and contribute to the ways in which people deny and exclude each other. We look at the vast needs of the world and all its peoples, and realize that we cannot separate our own well-being from the well-being of others. Their needs are our needs. Their concerns are our concerns. If they are suffering we are suffering. If they are the victims of injustice then we also are affected. We come to realize that it is impossible to completely enjoy the giftedness of life if others are denied the essentials that we take for granted.

We also come to recognize that our own actions may be causing others pain: leaving the tap running when you clean your teeth; not bothering to recycle empty bottles; reliance on cars and aeroplanes; building regulations that allow people to get away with houses that consume and waste energy. And so it goes on. The more people truly see and honour each other, the more they are moved to speak out against the self-seeking apathy that allows so many of us to pretend that the concerns of the world are not ours.

The noise of the world all around you all too easily drowns out the voice of God that is within you. Its seductive clamour reels you in. You are harangued at every turn: someone making a pitch, someone trying to sell you something that you didn't know you needed, that you never wanted until its shiny newness offered the missing extra that will render you desirable. 'Buy me, love me, use me' the world pleads in shrill insistence.

By learning to sit still, slow down, by discerning when to shut up and when to speak out, you learn to travel through life differently. You take notice of the quiet voice within rather than the strident voices around. You start longing for stillness, seeking out silence, cherishing the present, striving for simplicity.

All this brings new delight in friendships and relationships. We stop seeing other people only in terms of what they can do for us. We appreciate them for who they are and our lives are richer as a result. Other people are no longer the walk-on parts in the universal drama of our lives, but fellow pilgrims in whom we can discover community, and to whom we can give and from whom we can receive affirmation, encouragement and wisdom.

There is new delight and purpose in the mundane and the ordinary things of life. Making tea becomes a treat. Travelling to work an adventure. Cooking a meal a voyage of discovery. Eating it a perilous pleasure. Daisies in the lawn become invitations to explore the creativity of God. Standing still in the dark we can see everything. And we discover that the tarmac in the slow lane is laced with gold.

Like a mountaineer inching his way up the sheer, vertical plane of a cliff we carve some stillness out of all the busyness and then discover that despite the clamour and demand it is possible to be still in the midst of everything, finding an inner peace that upholds and sustains us even when the pressures outside seem intolerable.

And lest we start believing that this is some fantastic achievement and that we are, after all, a fairly sensational sort of people, remember that in discovering this stillness – this slowness, this silence – we have discovered God. We have found God's presence within ourselves and in everything else around us. This increases our sense of wonder and we long to gorge ourselves on life. Everything is so beautiful.

At the same time, it is possible to experience a deeper appreciation of what you already have. But you don't need to possess it. You can appreciate it as another interconnected part of this astonishing creation that God's love has willed into being. You can appreciate it because you no longer place yourself at the centre. You are part of it, and for this you give thanks.

All this leads to a certain sort of prayer which Christians call adoration. It is perhaps the highest prayer of all. It is a way of looking at the world that is more than thanksgiving – although this is how it begins. The more you live thankfully, the more you discover a well of thankfulness that is already present in your heart. And the more you draw from it, the deeper the well becomes and the more satisfying the waters.

It is a way of loving. We adore God, disclosed to us in the wonders of everyday living. We enjoy the little things that make up our day. We adore the world and ache to see the beautiful harmony of the world upheld, and to reverse the trends of selfishness and greed, which continue to maintain that poverty and injustice are a sad inevitability, rather than the deliberate downside of our own riches. It is as if we are seeing the world with the eyes of God.

By sitting still for a few moments you discover that the tea tastes nicer when you have warmed the pot.

A DAY OFF AT LAST

Heaven is much too serious a place for work. It will
be all dance and play there.

C. S. Lewis

One of the great joys of being a dad is reading bedtime stories to
your children. You are forced to stop. The stories themselves put
you back in touch with childhood. And every story is accompanied
by a cuddle. What could be better?

In particular I have enjoyed reading Winnie the Pooh. However, I
have never managed to get to the end of the final chapter of *The
House at Pooh Corner* without weeping. It is achingly sad. This is
the chapter where Christopher Robin is about to go away to
school. After a farewell gathering he takes Pooh to an enchanted
place on the other side of the forest and tries to explain to him the
strange mysteries of growing up. But these are things he doesn't
quite understand himself, so he struggles to find the words that
will convey the rapid changes that lie ahead of him and the
enormity of the things he must leave behind.

As they walk along they chat about this and that, and Christopher
Robin asks Pooh what he likes doing best in all the world. Pooh
begins to say that eating honey is the best thing, but then he

reflects that there is 'a moment just before you began to eat it which was better than when you were, but he didn't know what it was called'. This seems to me to be a profound reflection borne of a real appreciation of the glorious giftedness of life. Some things are so beautiful, so satisfying, so desirable that the anticipation of receiving them is almost better than the receiving itself. Though the wonder of the receiving overwhelms you, there is something uniquely special about dwelling in the moment of anticipation.

There are certain pieces of piano music that give me this feeling. I am, of course, thinking of particular pieces of music – one of Chopin's nocturnes or Mendelssohn's *Songs without Words*. I am thinking of these pieces because they were played by my mother and seem to have accompanied me throughout my life. But it is not just the music I am thinking of, nor the memories the music evokes, but the sense of wonder that music is made up of the notes themselves and also the silence between the notes. And all these are both given in the writing down of the music and endlessly re-created in the different interpretations of each individual performance. If it is a piece you know well, there is, sometimes, in a new interpretation, a moment of tremulous expectation when the pianist pauses for a fraction of a second that can seem like an eternity, and the anticipation of what is to come, that single longed-for note, enhances and heightens the beauty when at last it is played.

Can the whole of my life be such a moment of ecstatic antic- ipation, waiting to hear the completion of the music I already know: the music of creation that made me, that plays in the uni- verse around me, that beckons from the God who composed me?

Most of the time the answer must be no, I am simply too bound up with my own ambitions and trivialities, too self-centred and self-seeking to enter into the possibilities that are right in front of me. But sometimes it is different. That is all that this book has been about – the sustaining glimpses of these differences, and the hope that they might multiply, changing my life and changing the world. Or, to put it another way, when you start to live with the appreciation that everything you experience in this life comes from God, then you can live each moment as an anticipation of the delight that awaits you when you see God face to face.

But Pooh has an even deeper wisdom to impart. There are some things even better than the anticipated delight of eating honey. It was being with the people he loves. He eventually concludes that the very best thing in all the world is for 'Me and Piglet going to see You [Christopher Robin], and You saying "What about a little something?" and Me saying, "Well, I shouldn't mind a little something, should you, Piglet," and it being a hummy sort of day outside, and birds singing'.

Here Pooh adds to his first observation that true happiness can be found as much in the anticipation of delight as in the delight itself, by saying that this delight can only truly be enjoyed when it is in the company of others.

I can't read this passage without thinking of the Christian Eucharist: the service of Holy Communion, which is at the heart of Christian worship. Here bread and wine are broken and shared in remembrance of the meal Jesus shared with his friends on the night before he died. The meal, however, signifies more than fellowship. It is enacted parable, indicating the meaning of his death on the cross. Like the bread that is broken and the wine poured out, Jesus' body will be broken on the cross and his blood shed. These will be the sufferings he faces before his risen life can be shared.

In the Christian Eucharist we receive the life of Christ. His life is shared with us. The breaking of the bread and the pouring of the wine remind us of his actions and draw us into the meaning of the cross. Christians believe that God uses the bread and wine to feed those who come to him in faith. The invitation to share the bread and wine, and the communion itself, anticipates that eternal moment of God's eternity when we will dwell in the presence of God and gather at the heavenly banquet. In other words it is a meal held in the company of friends, in which we receive the life of heaven that the meal anticipates. Indeed, the word 'company', and the word 'companion' that is derived from it, come from the French meaning, literally, 'one with whom we break bread'.

It is then Christopher Robin's turn to answer his own question. And his answer leads us back to the central message of this book and to the great Sabbath rest that the Jewish and Christian faiths describe as the climax of God's creation. 'What I like *doing* best', says Christopher Robin, 'is Nothing.'

'How do you do Nothing?' asks Pooh, after he had wondered for a long time. 'Well, it's when people call out at you just as you're going off to do it, "What are you going to do, Christopher Robin?" and you say "Oh nothing," and then you go and do it. It means just going along, listening to all the things you can't hear, and not bothering.'

Listening to the things you can't hear. Seeing the things you can't see. Loving the things you can't feel. Here we are very close to the topsy-turvy absurdity of Christian faith. For at its heart, the Christian faith has a conviction that the deepest reality abides in those things that cannot be seen or heard. Faith itself, says the New Testament, 'is the assurance of things hoped for, the conviction of things not seen' (Hebrews 11.1).

The world around us is real, it is beautiful and God can be found in it. But it will pass away. This is what is known about all created things. They live and they die. The earth makes its constant orbit round the sun and from it receives the energy needed for life. But even the sun will burn itself out, and this universe, which is inexorably expanding, will, one day, when time itself ceases to be, contract upon itself and be no more. This living and dying is all around us. You see it in the pattern of the seasons, in all the tiny deaths that make up human life, and in the vast, aching tragedies of individual lives lost or broken. You cannot escape it. It is with you every day and it waits for you at the day that will be your last.

But there is another, deeper reality. Not a reality that is separate from what you see and feel, but behind it and between it; a reality that has no beginning or end, that is uncreated, and upon which everything else rests. It is quite possible to go through all of life not noticing this reality. It is quite possible to doubt it and disbelieve it. There is plenty of evidence to suppose that such a claim is wistful madness. Earthquakes, cancer, human hatred, prejudice, all do more than enough to chip away at any hope that the universe may be lovable. And yet this hope persists. It lives cheek by jowl with misery and danger, and despite the tremendous capacity of human freedom to create and destroy, human beings go on hoping.

People go on hoping because the things that are unseen, the things that are felt and believed, seem somehow to be more certain. Through them we glimpse the possibility of God, and we dare to hope that beyond the last breath of the last moment of this life, there is something else. This something else is called the eternal presence of God. It is a presence that has created and sustains the universe. It is a presence that awaits us at the end. When we try to capture it, it eludes us. This is not a God who can be pinned down, or clung to, or constrained by definitions and dogmas. Many good people, in trying to define and capture the presence of God, have ended up destroying it. The rules and regulations of religion have often suffocated the life of the Spirit. Nevertheless, the great religions of the world teach us to reach beyond ourselves. Their definitions and dogmas are not pigeon-holes but growbags; well-fertilized soil in which faith and hope can grow. And the Christian way – this religion that is not a religion – this strange, participative drama in which the invisible God becomes flesh, offers an invitation to a different sort of living in which every moment is a foretaste of glory and an opportunity to discern and celebrate the presence of God.

In the Creation story at the beginning of the Bible we are told that God laboured for six days in the great work of creation but on the seventh day, seeing the goodness and harmony of all that had been made, rested. This seventh day is the day God has hallowed. It is a day of rest and celebration that is a gift in creation. It is also the fourth of the Ten Commandments: Remember the Sabbath day and keep it holy.

For us, in the busy Western world, any sense of a special day of rest and re-creation has long since disappeared. Sunday is just like any other day. The boundaries between the different days of the week, the seasons of the year, and even, nowadays, between night and day, have been eroded. This brings a terrible loss. People are deprived of the rhythms and patterns that shape life. And with this, the pressure to be busy and productive increases. There is less time for family, less time for leisure, less time for the re-creation, which is the purpose of leisure.

Christians and non-Christians alike may crave for a return to a more ordered rhythm to the week, but it seems unlikely that this will come about in the near future. Therefore, rather than fighting a rearguard action to keep Sunday special, it might be better to consider how you can build some Sabbath time into the schedules and rhythms of the life you have. These are the disciplines of slowing down and shutting up that were explored in the last chapter. They are a recovery of Sabbath, the creation of a place of rest where joy and contentment can flourish.

So let's spend more time listening to the things we can't hear and therefore coming closer to the things we cannot see. This will not only prepare us for heaven, it will enable us to live the life of heaven, the true Sabbath, here on earth.

In doing nothing; in taking rest and play seriously; in unmasking the illusion that meaning and value can only be found in busyness and so-called productivity; in learning to cherish the present moment, we discover that God can best be found in the silences between the notes; in what is written between the lines. Not through our effort, or hard work, or even our goodness, but in those moments of forgetfulness, of sleeping and dreaming, when we are suddenly caught unawares by the wild and mysterious beauty of the world. This is the Sabbath rest that the Christian Scriptures promise: a place of homecoming and a place of creativity.

So switch off the TV; put this book down; shut your eyes; breathe deeply; dream; do nothing but listen to the things you can't hear. Nurture your inner slob. You might even find you begin to pray – not by saying a lot of stuff to God, but by enjoying the intimacy of God's presence and the fragile beauty of each passing moment.

To put it another way: don't just do something, sit there!

A FINAL THOUGHT

> There are these rare moments when musicians
> together touch something sweeter than they've ever
> found before in rehearsals or performance, beyond
> the merely collaborative or technically proficient,
> when their expression becomes as easy and graceful
> as friendship or love. This is when they give us a
> glimpse of what we might be, of our best selves, and
> of an impossible world in which you give everything
> you have to others, but lose nothing yourself.
>
> Ian McEwan, *Saturday*

Nowadays many people live pressured and anxiety-driven lives.
Everything seems drained of purpose. All around us there is stress,
breakdown and disappointment. People feel unfulfilled. There was
a time when life seemed to promise something, but it has slipped
out of view and nothing seems able to bring it back. The only
purpose left is survival, a half-satisfied life that salvages bits of
comfort here and there.

Some people hope for a win on the lottery. This would indeed bring
great material benefit, but the vain hopes on offer carry just a very
large dose of what is causing the hurt in the first place; another
way of finding happiness at everyone else's expense.

And, of course, most of us don't win. Most of us just go on from day to day feeling frustrated by the transience of life, confused and confounded by failed loving and broken relationships, raking regretfully over a past of lost opportunities, and fearful for a diminishing future. Life slips through our fingers, and we settle for compromise, resigned to the loss of any hope we may have had, refining our well-honed cynicism for anyone with an alternative vision, and grimly awaiting the unwelcome finality of death. This is the reality of so many lives at the beginning of this twenty-first century. The ravages of the last century have blown all optimism away.

But all this can be changed. And in the twinkling of an eye, and without effort, or at least not dependent on some superior intelligence or skill. It just requires an honest recognition of who we are – individual, social and creative beings made in the image of a creator God. There is a purpose to life, but it can only be found in community with God, which also means community with each other.

A good analogy (though all analogies are woefully incomplete) would be a key and a lock. A key without a lock is complete in itself. It cannot be a better key. There is not any part of the key missing. It is just that until it is placed in the lock and turned it never fulfils what it was created to achieve. Likewise, we are made for community with God.

Or think of the two staves of a piano score: the bass line played on its own is beautiful, and heard in isolation gives the appearance of being complete. But when the treble line is played as well, the bass line is not obliterated and is still heard clearly, but now in a more beautiful and satisfying harmony – so beautiful that you would never consider playing it in isolation again. It is a new and transcendent experience of what already is. It is made complete, and at the same time is completely transformed, by the additional music. So it is when your life is played in partnership and harmony with the God who is your composer.

You can be half-happy without God, half-satisfied, half-fulfilled, half-complete. Though increasingly this is not how you feel. The glass feels half-empty, not half-full. But until you hear a whisper of the melody that God plays to accompany and fulfil the music of your life, then there will always be that nagging feeling that something is missing. Not a hole in your life waiting to be filled, but another dimension waiting to be heard and experienced.

When I'm getting stressed at home, or when those nagging mid-life anxieties are pinching my heart, my teenage son often looks at me with weary opprobrium and tells me to chill out. Or else he tells me to take deep breaths. Or he says, 'Relax, Dad, you'll live longer.' Usually, his dismissive tone and the misplaced confidence of his youth propel me into a rage. But now, of course, I realize he is right. I do need to slow down. I do need to chill out. I do need to take deep breaths. I may not live longer if I relax, but I will certainly live better, and I will certainly live differently. If I stop for a bit I will see my life differently, I will see the world differently, and I am more likely to be in tune with God and hear the music of his love, and therefore be more in tune with myself.

And so I will discover the meaning in life. The meaning that so much of my conscious anxiety conceals from me. I will find the purpose in the slowing down, in the deep breaths, in the chilling out. I will find that God does have a purpose for my life. But it is a purpose that cannot be measured by human achievements, but by developing a capacity to dwell in the present moment – to rest, play and enjoy. And this dwelling in the present moment will not be the phoney feel-good philosophy that says 'today is the first day of the rest of your life' for I know that yesterday was the first day, and today I must live my life not fretting about what happened, but being reconciled to it. I will learn from my past and I will move into a future that is a sacred series of precious moments, each disclosing the presence and beauty of God. Both my past and my future meet here. They are paths that lead to and from my own presence into God's eternal presence. And if I am able to dwell completely in just one of the many moments that I trust still lie before me then I will have tasted heaven, I will have heard the music of God and discovered myself in that great hymn of praise; and I will be better prepared for what is to come, both beyond this life and in this life's subsequent moments.

I will find that I can pray: not just the dogged, disciplined prayer of carving out times of reflection amid the busyness of life. I will laugh and cry at the madness and joy in the world. I will discover an ability to delight and wonder in the people and things that are around me, and wish them well, and respect them with such loving attentiveness that I may even start to burn with God's desire for a just and equitable ordering of the world.

I will love myself as a precious, vital and beautiful thread in the tapestry of God's creation; but I will also recognize that I am just one among many, and that my well-being cannot be separated from the well-being of the whole. I will glory in the astonishing fact that I have been created at all. I will recognize that the possibility of 'me', of cells combining into life to form this particular one-off arrangement of the human pattern, is incredible and unrepeatable and profoundly beautiful: present in the mind of God from the very first moment of creation.

And then I will lie back and be at peace with myself. With any luck, and if there isn't anyone about, I will probably doze off and enjoy a barely earned forty winks. And I will be smiling.

> Jesus said, I thank you Father that you have hidden these things from the wise and the intelligent and have revealed them to infants; yes, Father, for such was your gracious will . . . Come to me, all you that are weary and are carrying heavy burdens and I will give you rest. Take my yoke upon you and learn from me, for I am gentle and humble in heart and you will find rest for your souls. For my yoke is easy, and my burden is light.
>
> *Matthew 11.25, 26, 28-30*

A FEW THINGS I HAVE FOUND HELPFUL

Three films to make you feel good about being alive

Babette's Feast

Cinema Paradiso

Ferris Bueller's Day Off

Three books to release your inner slob

Generation X, a novel by Douglas Coupland (St Martin's, 1991)

Staying Alive, a collection of poems edited by Neil Astley (Bloodaxe, 2002)

Health, Money and Love: And why we don't enjoy them, an enjoyably challenging look at the Christian faith by Robert Farrar Capon (Eerdmans, 1990)

Three pieces of music to inspire your inner dreams

Chopin's *Nocturnes*

Philip Glass's *Violin Concerto*

John Tavener's *The Protecting Veil*